Met Police London:

Terrorism, Murder, and Police Corruption

Revelations of a London Detective Inspector

By Robert Jones BSc (hons)

Contents

Introduction

As a new detective constable fresh out of the Metropolitan Police Detective Training School, I joined West Ham CID on Monday, 7th October 1985. This was the day after the Broadwater Farm riots in Tottenham, during which PC Keith Blakelock was murdered by a gang of rioters. By then, I had been a police officer in the Met for five years.

Six months later, I would meet the greatest challenge of my life when I decided to take covert action against my supervisor. He was a detective sergeant, and I was unexpectedly confronted with his seriously corrupt behaviour. My actions resulted in his conviction at the Old Bailey and a term of imprisonment. The ramifications of my honesty were to change my life forever.

Four years later and now a detective sergeant, I encountered serious police corruption on the Flying Squad at Rigg Approach, the East London branch of the organisation. Here, I was threatened, assaulted, and subject to extremely coercive management practices. The name 'Rigg

Approach' has become synonymous with 'Police Corruption'. Many of their detectives were subsequently imprisoned for corruption.

Following this, I spent over six years on the Anti-Terrorist Branch at New Scotland Yard. I took the lead nationally regarding police video evidence. The IRA referred to me as the 'Video King', and I frequently worked in the north and south of Ireland in very hostile environments.

Upon promotion to detective inspector and being posted to Haringey Borough, I developed a unique police CCTV system. This system was responsible for the arrest and conviction at court of over two hundred criminals for offences such as murder, attempted murder, serious assaults, and many muggings. Over nine hundred crimes were solved. This successful police CCTV system was eventually destroyed by serious mismanagement committed by a Metropolitan Police commissioner.

During my twenty-five years of police service and through my own efforts, I have solved four separate murders.

I was sponsored during my police service to study for a degree and achieved a BSc (hons).

I have a younger brother and sister, who both live in London. My brother was principal cello in the Orchestra of the Royal Opera House, Covent Garden. My sister is the youngest of the three of us and is a devoted mother to her two children. My father was a former RAF pilot and became an airline captain with British Airways. His postings to various airports took us around the country. I believe that living in different areas in the country was beneficial to our upbringing. It gave us a greater insight into life and was character-forming for all of us. As a family, we have lived in Shrewsbury, Knutsford, Jersey, London, Guildford, and Manchester.

Prior to my police service, I was a fireman in Greater Manchester for four years and a commissioned officer in the Royal Navy for two years.

I have a son and a daughter from my first marriage and a further son and daughter from my second marriage.

During my career with the Metropolitan Police, I was frequently referred to as 'the biggest loose cannon in the Met'. I don't regard that as an insult; the Met would have benefitted from more 'loose cannons' in my opinion, particularly in the higher ranks.

To save any embarrassment, I have not named the officers I worked with in this book.

I have given the exact dates of events wherever possible.

I have referred to the London Metropolitan Police Service as 'the Met' throughout this book as it is a recognised abbreviation.

The Met is by far the largest police force in the UK. At the time of writing in 2021, it comprised 32,000 police officers and 10,000 civilian support staff. The population of London as of 2021 is about nine million.

I have not written this book to simply record the events of my police career for the reader's entertainment; instead, I have tried to enlighten the reader as to the complexities, dilemmas, and frustrations police officers face. These challenges amount to more than just risks to their lives. I have often been asked how I coped with the stress of dealing with criminals. My response was not expected: I told them I would rather deal with criminals than the arrogance, vanity, and incompetence of most senior officers promoted way beyond their capabilities. In my experience, the higher a police officer's rank, the lower the number of arrests they have ever made. The public quite rightly judge police officers by the number of arrests they make. Is that not what they are there for? Arrest numbers have nothing to do with promotion assessments; the police promotion process is not interested in this factor.

I see the lack of competent, experienced, and independent leaders within the police far more damaging than cuts in police numbers.

School Days

I was educated at the Royal Grammar School in Guildford, Surrey. The school was founded in 1547 by King Edward VI. This was a state grammar school when I was a pupil, and selections were based on merit. Today, it is fee-paying.

Terry Jones from *Monty Python* was head boy at the school during the early 1960s. England cricketer and television commentator Bob Willis, a few years older than me, was a pupil while I was there. I remember watching him practice his bowling skills in the cricket nets, and it was predicted that he one day might play for Surrey County Cricket Club! Dave Benest was in my class and became the commanding officer of the Second Battalion of the Parachute Regiment.

The original 16th century stone building is still used as part of the school for teaching and is prominently situated on High Street. The upper floor has a medieval chain library with original books from that period.

My nickname at the school was 'Stan'. This was perhaps a rather odd name for a teenager. I went to school with fellow pupil Andrew Hall, who lived near me. He became a star in the BBC comedy series *Butterflies* with Nicholas Lyndhurst, Geoffrey Palmer, and Wendy Craig. He also starred in the *Coronation Street* television series. He was never the best timekeeper, and we often arrived late for school assembly. This required us to hide under desks while prefects searched for us. In those days, the headmaster used the cane on those who transgressed. Fortunately, I never suffered that fate.

I played for the school Rugby 2nd XV and occasionally the 1st XV. I was one of the first in my school class to have a girlfriend—my school was all boys, and girls were difficult to find!

As pupils, we were pushed quite hard academically. It was normal to have a least three hours of homework every night. The school was managed on public school lines. The teachers wore black gowns and mortarboards to signify their degree status. Pupils were only known by their surnames to the teachers. To this day, I still refer to my former classmates by their surnames. I was fortunate that I lived less than a mile away from the school. Other pupils had to travel for many miles.

It was not unusual for pupils to be assaulted or insulted once outside school, and we were often regarded as elitist and snobbish. Our school uniform was distinctive, which did not help. One day at lunchtime, I left the school and went for a walk in the town. We were forbidden to do this. I cannot remember why I did it, but I suspect it was to escape from the formality of school. I walked along High Street, then turned right into Swan Lane. This was a narrow lane, free from traffic and with shops on either side. Five young men and two young women wearing Chelsea football scarves walked past me from North Street in the opposite direction. I thought nothing more about it until one of the men came up to me and accused me of hitting him. I had done nothing of the sort. Why would I attack five young men on my own? The others surrounded me and told me they would 'sort me out' for this. They were obviously picking on me because I was on my own, in school uniform, and they saw it as fun. They were thugs.

I asked one of their young women if they were impressed with their men picking on someone on his own. She just looked blank. At this point, all the men jumped on me, and I fell to the ground under their many kicks and punches. A member of the public intervened. He emerged from an adjacent shop that sold men's clothes and said loudly that no one was to put the boot in while he was around. He pulled them off me. He was well over six feet tall and had the build of a bouncer. My attackers then disappeared. I should have thanked him; I was probably too embarrassed to do so.

The next morning, in school assembly, my French teacher announced to the school that he wanted the pupil who had been involved in the fight to step forward and admit his involvement. Apparently, several members of the public had reported the incident to the school. I remained silent. Nothing would have been achieved by admitting my 'guilt'. Perhaps this was why we were forbidden to leave the school grounds during lunchtime?

I think that this and other assaults caused me to consider a police career.

Although I stayed on at the school to sit my 'A-Level' examinations at eighteen years of age, I felt as though I had grown out of being at school a couple of years before then. I think my irritation with school life spilled over a few times regarding the school staff. One incident involved the secretary, who organised the day-to-day running of the school. She was a middle-aged woman, who was always quite aggressive and rude towards pupils. One day, following her anger towards me over a minor incident, I told her to her face exactly what I thought of her attitude. I didn't hold back in my condemnation of her. That afternoon, she burst into the classroom and demanded to know if 'Jones' was in class. I was to immediately report to the headmaster when the lesson had ended. The rest of the class gasped, knowing that I was likely to be caned; they had heard about my confrontation with her.

At the end of the lesson, I made my lonely way to the headmaster. The school secretary was at her desk adjoining his office. Immediately upon seeing me, she stepped out from behind her desk and opened the headmaster's study door. She almost gleefully informed him in her matriarchal voice that 'Jones' was here to see him. She then glared at me before stepping out of his study.

He told me to close the door. I expected the worst. I remained standing, and the headmaster remained seated. Without once looking up at me and with his head slightly bowed, he told me that I really ought to treat his staff with respect. He said all this as he tried to stop laughing! He said that some staff can be difficult, but it was no excuse for my behaviour. He was still trying to stop laughing! He then dismissed me from his office. As I left his study, the school secretary again glared at me, but this time, I sensed disappointment in her eyes. She had obviously been hoping that I would be caned. This was a lesson in life for me: that it is possible to stand up for yourself against your superiors and still survive. It's a lesson for all of us.

Fate works in mysterious ways. I was almost killed in a motorbike accident very shortly after this. Perhaps the school secretary put a curse on me. It happened at about 10 pm on Guildford High Street near my school. I was a passenger when a friend of mine lost control of his 500cc machine, crossed over the road, and hit an oncoming car head-on. I remember that the car we hit was a Triumph Spitfire and that we were travelling at about 50 mph towards it. (We never travelled anywhere at less than 50 mph). The last thing I remembered was that I felt helpless about the impending impact and that there was absolutely nothing I could do about it. I fleetingly considered that the consequences of this impact would result in great physical pain for me. I have no further memory of this crash.

The ambulance crew found me. I was quite some distance away, having been thrown off the bike and into the air by the collision. I was unconscious, and my crash helmet had split open. I was put into the ambulance with my friend. He told me afterwards that he thought, from the look on my unconscious face, that I was dead. I woke up in Guildford hospital the next day, suffering from a severe concussion and a few minor cuts. I kept losing consciousness for the next two weeks. My friend survived with a gashed leg. Unsurprisingly, the motorbike was written off and sold for scrap. Crash helmets were optional at that time—without one, I would have been killed.

I was sixteen when I bought my first pint of beer at a pub. It was The Ship at Saint Catherine's village on the outskirts of Guildford. A few friends were in the pub car park, and we shared the beer. I lived nearby on Guildown Road. By now, I often hosted parties at home for fellow pupils with the aim of attracting as many girls as possible. I had developed a taste for beer and the opposite sex. What could possibly go wrong?

I was put off joining the police for many years by a couple of unpleasant experiences when I was a teenager living in Guildford. One such experience with the police occurred when I was about sixteen. I was helping a school friend push his motorbike up the steep Guildford High Street in Surrey one Saturday afternoon. It had broken down, and we were heading for his home nearby. Two police officers approached us. They wore peaked caps, and they had probably seen us from their patrol car and decided to question us. They spoke to my friend first and asked about his ownership of the bike. They were unnecessarily aggressive, I thought. Perhaps there had been a misunderstanding? I tried to assist by explaining what had happened. At this point, one of the officers turned to me and told me to "keep 'effing quiet". He also said that if they wanted to hear from me, they would "'effing let me know." My attitude to the police changed at that moment, from being supportive to one of hostility. We had done nothing wrong, but as far as these officers were concerned, we were there to be verbally abused, and they had absolutely no respect for us.

Another incident, again involving Surrey Police, was the attitude of a detective after I had been assaulted on the way home from school. I had been punched violently in the mouth by one of three adult men for no reason as they walked past me on the pavement. Nothing was said to me by any of them. It was entirely unprovoked and random. They then ran off. A knuckle-duster was probably used, as my lower lip was split in two and my front teeth were broken. The front of my shirt, tie, and blazer were covered in my blood. I continued to walk home and, once there, called the police. The detective who attended said dismissively after looking at me, "I've seen worse". He then walked away. Was he trying to impress me with his worldly experience of injuries? That was his only comment to me. It was as if I was to blame for bothering him.

Nobody was arrested for this crime. This one act of pointless savagery affected me for many years. I was to endure over six months of painful dental treatment. When I became a police officer nearly ten years later in the Met, I was able to draw upon those experiences with Surrey Police and always tried to be particularly careful and considerate in my dealings with teenagers.

Four Years with Greater Manchester Fire Service

After leaving school, I tried a very brief career in a bank. It was certainly not for me! I then decided to do something that was as far away from an office environment as possible: I became a fireman in the Greater Manchester Fire Service for the next four years. The Fire Service attracted me as I saw it as a huge challenge and beyond anything I had ever experienced. The training was held at a bleak ex-military base in Chorley, Lancashire. It was the most physically demanding period of my life and lasted for four months.

I was married on the third day of my course; the day had been arranged long before the date of the course had been decided. The venue was at a hotel in Altrincham and had been booked both for the wedding breakfast and the reception later that day. I had to ask the commanding officer for leave, and he granted me a twenty-four-hour pass! My wedding night was in the hotel, and I had to leave at 5 am to be on time for the course. My honeymoon was delayed for four months. Two months after the honeymoon, my wife gave birth to our son. I bought my first home. It was a small, modern end of terrace house.

My first fire station was located in the town of Sale on the outskirts of Manchester. I saw this career as being the most exciting job in the world. Our shift was made up of real characters and the types you knew you could depend on in any emergency. The *esprit de corps* was high, and we also mixed socially after work. This entailed drinking the finest of Manchester ales: breweries such as Robinsons, Holts, and Boddingtons will always be remembered. Sale fire station was close enough to home for me to cycle to work on my old school bike.

Within my first two weeks at the fire station, our crew attended an extremely demanding emergency with a risk to life. The station alarm sounded, and we were told to go to a location near the M62 motorway as a lot of smoke had been reported by members of the public. We made our way at speed towards the location. As we got closer, I could see a vast quantity of thick black smoke heading skywards from a blazing petrol tanker. The tanker had overturned on its side on a slip road joining the M62 and had caught alight. Masses of flames gushed from the ruptured tanks. The tanker was on the slip road at the top of a grassy slope about forty feet above us, but we could not access the slip road with our fire engine—it would mean a detour of at least fifteen minutes to reach it. We could only go on foot. I and my fellow recruit had to climb the steep embankment with our hoses to get to the fire.

Our fire engine was unique in that it carried a large tank of foam concentrate, which could be mixed with the 2,000 litres of water that we carried as standard. This mix created a blanket of foam. (Water on its own would have spread the flames and not extinguished it). Several other fire engines were already on the motorway but were helpless to do anything as they did not have the same foam equipment as us. I and the other recruit made our way over a high fence and up the slope, unreeling and joining up the heavy hoses as we did so. When we reached the same level as the tanker, the fierce heat from the flames hit us. The heat was of intensity far, far beyond anything I had experienced at training school. We had been told that the driver was trapped in his cab. We had to get closer so that the jet of foam could reach the tanker and smother the flames. In those days, firefighters were dressed in non-fire-resistant clothing.

Head protection was provided by a traditional cork helmet painted yellow, and there was no visor to protect the face from the heat, nor did we have breathing apparatus.

We shuffled along on our knees to provide some protection by getting below the burning heat layers. We gradually got closer. Somehow, we continued to direct the jet of foam onto the tanker. We both had our heads bowed down to protect our faces. I was, of course, concerned that the tanker might explode and bring a tragic yet spectacular end to both our short careers. Eventually, the fire began to lessen in severity, and we realised with relief that we had won.

When the flames died down, a senior fire officer approached us both. He was aware of the risks we had taken and that we were new recruits. He took us to the cab of the tanker as he thought it would be a good experience for us to see our first dead body. It was a sorry end and a disappointment as we thought the driver might have been saved, but we had done our best for him. We both received a commendation for our efforts.

I continued to attend fires and other emergencies over the following months. No call-out was ever the same, and the challenges could be immense.

I successfully completed a Breathing Apparatus (BA) course at Salford Fire Station. This qualification permitted me to enter burning buildings and risk my life while trying to save others. Firefighters have the job of running into buildings that everyone else is running out of. The smoke is usually so thick that it is impossible to see an inch in front of your face. The breathing apparatus provides the firefighter with compressed air from a tank on their back to breathe and is similar in many ways to the equipment a scuba diver uses. The biggest problem a firefighter faces in these situations apart from the fire is disorientation, getting lost in the building, and running out of air. Even a small room unknown to you can cause confusion in total darkness. Air supply is limited, and consumption increases drastically in high temperatures, high humidity, and during mental stress.

One afternoon while wearing breathing apparatus, I attended a fire in a house where the ground floor was so thick with smoke that I could not see anything at all. By shuffling along with my outstretched hand in front of me, I found a door. I turned the handle and emerged into what was clear air. I wiped the visor on my mask and saw that I was now in a pub with people standing around drinking and quite amazed to see me. I was also amazed to see them.

My days weren't all about fighting fires: I was also nominated to give talks at schools on firework safety throughout October and in the run-up to Bonfire Night. For a four-week period, I was my own boss. I was allowed a small station van to get me around and a few visual aids to illustrate the talks. I created my own timetable for school visits and composed my own notes for the talks. The hardest group of children to talk to were the five-year-olds, as I was never quite sure if I was getting my message across. Still, the teachers would reinforce what I had to say to the kids afterwards.

I visited a secondary school, where I intended to talk to the sixteen-year-old pupils. I saw this age group as being able to provide supervision at any bonfire they attended. On arrival at the school, I met with the headmaster in his study. He welcomed me and showed me the way to the classroom, where I was to give my talk. I followed him through the school for a minute or so. We walked up a few steps into a darkened area. At this point, a large set of curtains opened, and I found myself on a stage facing six hundred pupils and about thirty teachers. The headmaster introduced me to the audience and walked off the stage. I carried on as normal, but my presentation here was obviously not the same as for the five-year-olds. To keep their attention, I would randomly select a pupil to summarise a topic I had just covered. This certainly worked and kept their attention.

I later served at Broughton Fire Station near Salford, in Manchester. It was at that time the busiest fire station in Europe, with over 3,000 emergency calls per year and only one fire engine to respond. I had requested a transfer to Broughton as I wanted to gain further experience with a view to promotion.

I qualified at Bolton Fire Station to drive fire engines. In essence, this was a Heavy Goods Vehicle course. The first time I was nominated to drive the fire engine was on a Sunday. The shift started at 9 am and finished at 6 pm. I admit to being slightly on edge during that day while waiting for my first emergency call as a driver. Very unusually, the day was quiet, and there were no emergency calls. Just ten minutes before I was due to go off duty, the alarms around the fire station sounded. Now was my moment! I ran up to the fire engine and climbed into the driver's seat. The adrenalin was, of course, flowing, but I busied myself starting and monitoring the engine. I remembered to turn the flashing blue lights on! The rest of the crew were now in the back of the cab, getting dressed into their fire gear. The officer-in-charge then climbed aboard and into the seat next to me holding the fire message. Calmly, he told me that the call was categorised as 'Persons Reported'. This meant people were trapped in a burning building. This is the highest state of urgency for firefighters. By the time he had told me the address, I was already driving out of the fire station.

The important thing was to arrive at the emergency quickly and safely. This can be a tricky balance when lives are at stake. Traffic was busy, and there were crossroads to negotiate. Driving through a red light is hazardous, as not all motorists keep their ears and eyes open. I was the busiest member of the crew at this point, and the demands of this drive kept my mind highly focused. Two of the firemen in the back were putting on their breathing apparatus, which was not easy as the fire engine swayed through the traffic. As I turned right into a street, I saw at once that one of the terraced houses was 'well alight', to use a fire service term. I pulled up outside the house. We had made it, but my work was not done. I now had to man the pump at the rear of the fire engine and manage the flow of low and high-pressure water from our 2,000-litre tank. Without the rapid provision of water, the crew's efforts would be in vain. I also had to find a water hydrant to replenish the loss of water now being applied to the fire.

Shortly afterwards, I heard the good news that there was no one in the house to rescue, and we could now proceed to damp down the fire and try to save the house contents. On the way back to the station, none of the other firefighters mentioned my driving or complimented me. This meant I had done well—had I been at fault anytime during my drive, their criticism would have been blunt yet humorous.

Those four years were an amazing experience and will stay with me forever. Of interest, perhaps, Broughton Fire Station was haunted. Who by, we never knew, but many firefighters refused to work there, even temporarily. The ghost was known to us as 'George'. The fire engine was kept in what was referred to as the engine bay. This was an enclosed and tiled area with automatic doors, which were raised when an alarm was sounded. There were also lockers at the side assigned for personal fire gear. Sometimes at night, footsteps were heard as someone unknown walked around the engine bay, opening and slamming locker doors. It was known for firefighters to go into the engine bay and shout at 'George' to be quiet.

Often after a serious fire, we would stop our fire engine at the rear of one of the many Salford pubs, and the officer-in-charge would go in and buy each of us a pint of beer. He would emerge with a tray full of foaming glasses, and we would down them while gathered around our vehicle, swapping yarns. There was nothing better to quench a fireman's thirst—other than perhaps a second pint! I doubt this happens today.

During this time, I learned to fly at my own expense. I gained a private pilot's licence on a Cessna 150 aircraft, but the financial cost of being a father with a high-interest mortgage prevented me from any further flying. Many bills now had to be paid.

By this time, I was convinced that my career would be with the Greater Manchester Fire service. However, this was not to be.

Two Years with the Royal Navy (Fleet Air Arm)

I was happy as a fireman, but I saw a recruiting advert in a national newspaper that led me astray. The advert was for Harrier jump-jet pilots in the Royal Navy, flying from aircraft carriers. This certainly appealed to me. It was a very long shot, but I applied and hoped for the best. The selection procedure stretched over about six months, with leadership exercises, numerous interviews, and lengthy written tests. There were also various machines and devices to test mental and physical aptitude. At the conclusion of all this, there was a very rigorous medical examination.

Not only did I pass the officer and aircrew selection procedure at RAF Biggin Hill for pilot training, but I also passed observer training. The observer had the primary role of destroying Russian nuclear submarines. He also navigated the aircraft and coordinated the attack with friendly warships and aircraft. The observer also launched the weapon systems and was the captain of the aircraft during this deadly process. Despite my protests that I wanted to train as a pilot, it was decided by the powers that be that I should train as an observer instead.

My ten months officer training course was held at the Britannia Royal Naval College, Dartmouth, in Devon. The buildings were magnificent in design and sat on a hill overlooking the River Dart and the sea. My room was shared with four other officers under training. All four passed selection for pilot training but not observer training. Three of them became captains with major airlines. The fourth left the Royal Navy after gaining his pilot's wings. Several years later, he took part in a successful expedition to reach the South Pole on foot. I met him just before he set off. I was in the Met by now, and we had a few beers together. Their expedition was temporarily based at London Docklands. They bought an ice-breaking trawler and were about to head off south. They were successful in their challenging quest and achieved global fame.

I was in exceptional company with these four men. All were high achievers in life.

Within the first week, I had to take a standard Royal Navy swimming test. Dressed in overalls,

I was required to swim sixteen lengths of the college's Olympic-sized pool, tread water for three minutes, and retrieve a brick from the deep end. I failed as I could only swim a width and nothing else. I now had to reach this standard within three weeks. I spent every lunchtime practicing in the pool until I reached the necessary standard and passed the test.

We were not permitted to leave the college for the first six weeks. This was to prepare us for the constraints of life at sea.

After the six weeks, my wife and four-year-old son took up residence in a caravan a few miles away while I looked for more substantive accommodation. I had towed the caravan with my Vauxhall Viva van from Manchester on a leave day. Within the van were my wife, son, and dog; there were no Royal Navy married quarters available. A couple of weeks later, I was called upon to see a senior instructor, who was a lieutenant commander. He referred to me by my surname only, and he was very snobbish about this situation. He expressed his strong disapproval of my wife living in a caravan, and he made it clear he did not approve of a Royal Navy officer under training living in these circumstances. He sat behind his desk lecturing me while I remained standing.

About three weeks later, I found the type of

accommodation I had been all along looking for: a large bungalow with sixteen acres of land overlooking the sea. From my window, I could see the very modest rented accommodation of this instructor far below me in the village of Blackawton. Most of the instructors were egalitarian and not at all snobbish—he was the exception.

I and my colleagues on a free weekend often had a few beers back at my bungalow and, on occasion, had a few more beers in the Normandy Arms in nearby Blackawton. It was good at times to escape from the incessant, rigorous demands of training.

We had a leadership course of three days on Dartmoor. We slept at night on a rubber sheet under a piece of tarpaulin. One night, I had to keep watch for two hours while the other four slept. We were all very tired, having been kept on the move all day, having to carry heavy equipment for most of it. It was a clear night, and there was a full moon. Before long, the moon started to move around the sky. I was convinced it was really happening. I woke the others and told them to come and look at this amazing event. At this point, the moon stopped moving. It was an illusion caused by fatigue. The others were understandably not too happy at being woken over this!

The course at Dartmouth was intense and demanding. We were under the microscope for the whole of the course. There was an assessment almost every week throughout training as to my leadership qualities, academic ability, and physical fitness. The standards were high, and rightly so.

We were taught to march. I had a slight advantage as I had been taught this during my fire service training. However, military standard was much higher and, of course, involved a rifle and for us officers, a ceremonial sword. This was done on the parade ground in front of the main college building. Our instructors were petty officers (POs), equivalent in rank to sergeants in the army. Although we technically outranked them, they were in charge while we underwent training. They addressed us as 'sir', but we had to do as we were told. On one occasion, I made an error with my rifle drill. The petty officer told me, "You are an idiot, sir! What are you?" I replied, "I am an idiot, PO". He then said, "Now, be a good sir, and run around the parade ground twice with your rifle held above your head!" All this was done without the petty officer raising his voice. The Royal Navy had style.

We were taught to sail various craft. These ranged from a small sailing dinghy to a high-powered, eight-berth motorboat with twin diesel engines. I also spent a day on *HMS Porpoise*, a submarine. I was glad when that day was over. The submarine was based upon a WW2 German design and was extremely cramped. It used electric power when under the water; this made the boat quiet and difficult for the enemy to detect it. The captain wore a cravat and spun his cap around before viewing through the periscope, just as in the war films. Crew morale was high. The submarine service earned extra pay because of their demanding duties, as did pilots and observers.

The officer training was relentless. The hours were long, and there was constant pressure over the ten months to meet high standards. On several occasions, I was informed that I was likely to be streamed for pilot training rather than observer. It was expected that pilot assessment immediately after Dartmouth training would result in one or two officers being found unsuitable for further pilot training, and that I would fill this gap. I believed these promises at the time, but some months down the line, I discovered that they were false promises, as no observer was ever streamed into pilot training. Because of the special skills and abilities observers had, it was seen as a waste of resources to transfer an observer to pilot training. For the meantime, however, I was full of optimism that I would indeed be offered pilot training.

Prince Andrew joined for his officer training just before I graduated. He formed part of the Guard of Honour for my passing out parade. He enjoyed his time at Dartmouth, as did his older brother Prince Charles some years earlier.

Having successfully passed out from Dartmouth College, I spent three weeks on the Dartmouth Training Ship, *HMS Intrepid*. This was a Royal Marine Commando carrier that was also equipped with Wessex helicopters. We visited Gibraltar and Athens. The purpose was to give us a practical understanding of life aboard one of Her Majesty's warships. While at Gibraltar, I took part in the Rock Race. This involved running a race to the top of Gibraltar. I was certainly fit at that time!

I now had more training courses to successfully complete before I could commence observer flight training.

The first course involved familiarisation with the various specialist areas onboard a warship. One aspect involved the response of the warship to attack from an enemy aircraft. There was an assumption that only one aircraft at a time would attack the warship and not two simultaneously and from different angles. I asked how the warship would respond to an attack from two aircraft and was told that this would not happen. Sadly, two years later, during the Falklands war, the Argentine aircraft often attacked our warships in pairs from different angles with devastating effect.

One of the courses comprised learning how to escape from a helicopter that had crashed in the sea. I was strapped into a dummy helicopter with my colleagues as it was lowered into a very deep tank of water and turned upside down. Having undone my straps, I had to find my way out of the helicopter and reach the surface. About a week later, I was dropped into the English Channel while wearing flight clothing from a fast-moving launch. I had to wait for about fifteen minutes to be picked up by a helicopter. I have never been so cold in my whole life. It took me hours to get warm.

Part of this course was decompression awareness. If you gradually start to lose oxygen, you will eventually pass out and die. This can happen in an aircraft when damaged in flight at high altitude. To simulate this, I was placed in a sealed chamber, and the oxygen was gradually withdrawn. I was asked to carry out simple mathematical tasks and write them down on a clipboard over about ten minutes. I completed the task with ease. When I was released from the chamber and sat down, I looked at my written calculations on the clipboard. My calculations were correct at first, but gradually, they failed to make sense, and my writing became childlike and unintelligible. But my brain had not been aware of this extreme deterioration—as far as I was aware, everything was as normal. This is how aircraft can mysteriously crash when the crew are gradually starved of oxygen.

The most challenging assessment was the aircrew survival course. After two weeks of survival instruction, I had to survive for ten days without food and sleeping rough in the New Forest during February. These ten days simulated being shot down over enemy territory and being surrounded by hostile forces while trying to escape back to friendly forces.

A week before the survival course started, I became ill with a stomach bug. I could not eat. I should have reported sick, but I decided to persevere. The alternative was to be held back to recover and join a later course. I didn't want to do that and had loyalty to the members on my course. I ate little other than a couple of bowls of soup in the week before my survival course. By the time the course commenced, I closely resembled a skeleton.

Our first night on the survival course was spent in an inflatable rubber dinghy on a lake. There were twelve of us crammed into a dinghy designed to hold eight. We did not sleep. Our instructors shouted across to us in the early cold morning from the shore. They were cooking breakfast, and it included bacon: the denial of bacon when hungry was mental torture.

The next ten days on the course were a blur of fatigue, cold, and hunger. Our instructors had a caravan which they slept in at night. It was parked near wherever we ended up in the New Forest. I had an idea. At the next briefing from the instructors and while they were engaged, I would check their caravan for food. I sneaked away in the darkness and found their caravan. There was nobody nearby. I opened the door. The caravan was empty, but on the table was sliced white bread and a bowl of fruit. We had not eaten for four days. I 'liberated' a green apple and four slices of white bread. Back at the camp, I shared the bread and, with my survival knife, split the apple into four. I had a quarter. Immediately after eating this quarter of a green apple, my bowels woke up!

We had water bottles, but I had no urge to drink: I was always cold, and this made the thought of drinking water unattractive. As a result, I unknowingly started to suffer from dehydration, and my lips began to crack. I made myself take regular swigs of water, which cured the problem.

After about six days, we had an escape and evasion task. We were given a map reference to find a 'safe house' in the forest. The first one there would be given a bar of chocolate. A bar of chocolate was, to us in our starving state, the equivalent of steak and chips. It had been pouring rain for two days, and I was soaked. Patrols were also looking for us.

I was the leader of a group of four, and I had the map and compass. After about thirty minutes of following the map through the forest, I noticed out of the corner of my eye an enemy patrol hidden to our left about fifty yards away. I gathered the team together on the pretence of looking at the map. I told them we had been spotted and to bomb-burst on my count of four. We scattered, and I ran as fast and for as long as I could through the forest without once looking back. Eventually, I tired and looked back; the enemy patrol hadn't kept up with me. Deep joy! I was the first on the course to make it to the safe house. Within the house were five members of the course who had been captured earlier by the patrols. I asked for the bar of chocolate that I deserved and had been promised. I was told by the instructors that it was only a joke. I felt very tired and slightly dispirited at that point. But, I was the first to make it. Being first was better than chocolate.

For our final three days, we were permitted to light a fire and sleep in a makeshift shelter made of branches we had cut down. I found that trying to cut firewood was exhausting. The lack of food was fast weakening us.

At the end of the course, we were taken to a pub for soup and a bread roll. I had been dreaming of hot sausage rolls and onion sauce, but the bread roll would do for the time being. I was the only one not to lose weight on the course—my earlier illness ensured this would be the case.

After this, I started observer flight training with 750 Squadron at the Royal Naval Air Station Culdrose, near Helston in Cornwall. My training was on Handley Page Jetstream aircraft. The training exercises involved flying at almost ground level across the moors at high speed and conducting simulated attacks against shipping in the English Channel. My doubts of being suitable as an observer were confirmed: I found that I could not commit myself to the requirements expected. It was not for me.

After six months, I resigned from my commission. I was offered an alternative role as an air traffic controller, but I didn't see that as my future. There was an opportunity to apply to the RAF for pilot training—I was a 'known quantity', and the RAF was recruiting. However,

I would have had to go through initial training again, but this time with the RAF at Cranwell.

My time in the Royal Navy had come to an end. I had served for two years and left the Royal Navy as a sub-lieutenant. I had no regrets about either joining or leaving the Royal Navy. It had been an amazing experience.

At this point, I decided that the Metropolitan Police would provide an interesting alternative career. I felt that I now had the maturity and life experience to cope with the demands of policing. I also knew a serving Met police officer, who was the brother of a friend of mine in the Royal Navy. He was an intelligent guy and far superior to the police oafs I had previously met as a teenager in Surrey.

I joined the Metropolitan Police in October 1980. It was the biggest police force in the country by far, and I felt sure that I would find a role to suit me. I had a sense of fair play and felt I would have a real role in fighting the bad guys and making London safer. It sounds naive now, but I think that most police recruits join with this good intention in mind. I was twenty-six years old and married with a five-year-old son. Surprisingly, most of the recruits were not from London. Perhaps Londoners knew better?

The police selection process was quite

lengthy and lasted about four months. Much time was spent on background checks, and the medical examination was very thorough. My interview panel comprised three senior officers, and no difficult questions were asked. My background obviously suited, and I felt as though I had passed as soon as I was seated. In essence, we had what amounted to an informal chat and discussed career options within the Met.

So, I was now about to become a member of the Thin Blue Line!

Police Recruit Training Hendon Police College 1980-81

Looking back, my training as a recruit uniform constable was quite thorough. At first, it was an initial shock to be wearing the full police uniform, particularly when passing a mirror. Was this really me? I thought to myself. I was entering a closed society separate from the norm. How would I cope? What would be expected of me? Would I meet a racist, brutal, corrupt police world? There had been questions over police corruption in the 1970s, but I believed, perhaps naively, that the then Met commissioner, Sir Robert Mark, had eradicated all police corruption.

The training at Hendon was quite a pleasant surprise. Our class included recruits from varied backgrounds, but we all got on well somehow. I was class captain, which was like being a prefect at school. It was a slightly onerous role, but I coped without difficulty. Having a wife and child at home was financially demanding, and I rarely had the money to meet the class for a social drink. The college bar was not an attractive place anyway, and the local pubs were full of recruit police officers letting off steam. The college and its sports fields were situated on the old Hendon airfield, which dated back to the early 1900s. Across the road from the college was the Royal Air Force's aircraft museum.

We had our own individual rooms with washing facilities, a wardrobe, and a desk and chair. Our beds were made up for us and our rooms were also cleaned for us daily. For my Royal Navy training at Dartmouth, we had to make our own beds, share a room with four others, and have the room inspected to a high standard almost daily. My police training was very much more a civilian experience than a military one.

I owned an ex-Gas Board Vauxhall Viva van. The words 'Gas Board' could be faintly seen through the paint. As winter set in, the battery started to fail. I couldn't afford a replacement battery, so when I arrived at Hendon from home at about 6 am every Monday morning, I would disconnect the battery and carry it all the way to my room for charging. It was a walk of about a mile. On Friday evenings, I would carry it back to my car for the journey home to Oxfordshire. If the engine didn't start, I would find volunteers to push start the van and launch me on my way.

I was impressed with our sergeant instructors. Whether by design or accident, they taught us well. One day, our first instructor said we should always go in softly to an incident and be polite, even when dealing with aggressive, hardened criminals. He said that going in softly left room for manoeuvre. How right he was, and I have valued that approach to this day. During my police service, I have found that being polite to an arrested person really was of benefit. Even if he was indeed a hardened criminal, he was human. An offered cup of tea, even if refused, was helpful in us both getting along. If I was feeling generous (and in a good mood), I would include his solicitor.

The instructors also told us to ask questions, investigate, and never make assumptions. This stood me in good stead for the rest of my career. In other words, follow the evidence, and don't be side-tracked. Investigating a fatal car crash is essentially the same as investigating a murder – both involve establishing what happened before reaching conclusions.

Much of our instruction took place among the mock streets next to the college. We had simulated road traffic collisions and other incidents to deal with. There were also lessons in self-defence. We were taught how to disarm a man armed with a shotgun, pistol, or knife. The theory was sound, but I was not tempted to try it for real. There were instructions in marching and other parade ground skills. This was not difficult for me with my military background. It was a challenge for one or two who could not march in step. They would try so hard that both their arms would swing forwards and backwards as one while marching and their feet would shuffle, trying to keep step. It was hilarious.

The instructors were not racist. If they were, they hid it well. The reality was that I had only spoken to one Black person in my life before I joined the police. He was a trainee officer from an African country who sponsored him to receive training with the Royal Navy at Dartmouth. There was no discussion or lectures regarding racism in the police or in society. It was as if the subject was beyond any form of formal instruction. Perhaps they were right.

Our class was 100% white British, and about 10% were women. About 15% of the class resigned within the first week. Why join and then resign within a week? I thought to myself.

By today's standards, the instructors were sexist. Women who sucked their pens in class suffered merciless banter from the instructors. A woman flinched from diving from the top diving board during a swimming test; she was ferociously mocked until she jumped. It could be said that sexist banter ensured she passed the course. There were no complaints from the women about sexism, but society was perhaps different back then.

Hendon Police College comprised several tower blocks housing recruits under training. My room was on the eleventh floor, with a few floors above. It was known for recruits to walk around outside the block on the upper floors using the small window ledges. These ledges were about six inches deep. To do this – say, on the twelfth floor – required a strong nerve. At that height, the wind could be quite strong. I would like to say that I tried this, but I did not. As far as I know, there were no fatalities.

We only had one talk from a detective. He was a detective inspector with about twenty-five years' work experience in the Met. I later learned that Hendon Police College did not entirely approve of talks from experienced detectives as their contributions did not always follow the party line. I did note that our uniform instructors were not pro-CID. This detective inspector was a revelation to me. For instance, he spoke of an armed robber who had served a prison sentence of ten years but, upon release, was known to still be active in committing armed robberies. However, there was no evidence to arrest him. The only evidence available was his breach of firearms legislation when he once used an air rifle at a fair. The firearms legislation banned him after his prison sentence from using a firearm – an air weapon is a firearm. He ended up back in prison. To me, that showed lateral thinking and was to be commended.

The course was four months long, and my passing out parade was in February 1981. I approached this day with some trepidation. We were institutionalised on our course and had no idea what was waiting for us in the highly controversial Met. (I believe that this has all now changed, and recruits have an introduction during their training to actual policing).

My First Police Station Barkingside 1981–83

I was sent to Barkingside Police Station in 'J' District, in north-east London. I did not have a clue where this was and had to check on a wall map. I was provided with a married quarter in Leytonstone, East London. This was a two-bedroom flat; it was rent-free but not suited to us. There was no heating other than a coal fire, and we were cold.

To seek advice on the best local school for my five-year-old son, I spoke with the Home Beat police officer for the locality. I decided it would be best to move farther out and beyond the North Circular Road. Also, my car had been partially stripped by thieves when parked outside the police married quarters.

I managed to buy a semi-detached house in Barkingside. My pay barely covered the mortgage, food, and basic bills. I bought my car on a credit card for £600, and the repayments were vast due to over 30% interest rate charges. I was earning twice as much as I had in the Royal Navy as a sub-lieutenant. However, interest rates were now high, and the monthly mortgage and car loan payments consumed over half my take-home pay. UK inflation in 1980 was running at a high of 22% annually.

Barkingside Police Station was a plain and anonymous-looking building. It was built in the 1960s and situated on the high street. Its radio call sign was 'JB' or Juliette-Bravo in the phonetic alphabet. The famous Metropolitan Police blue lamp was close to the front entrance. There was an enclosed yard at the rear, where stolen cars were stored until reunited with their owners. There were sub-stations to Barkingside at Loughton, Woodford, and Chigwell. The chief superintendent's office was at Barkingside, as was the CID office for the Division. There were no entry codes on the outside doors; at that time, no unauthorised entry to a police station was ever anticipated or expected. Police officers did not wear body armour or stab vests; they did not carry body cameras or gas spray. High-visibility jackets were unheard of, and tasers had not yet been invented. We were issued a truncheon, but it was too clumsy to carry around. Most officers, including myself, did not carry one. We were always expected to wear a hat out of doors; this is no longer the case. We certainly did not look like night-club doormen.

The daily routine commenced with a formal parade of the officers engaged on that shift. It usually took place in the intelligence office. The parade was taken by the inspector, who allocated each officer a particular responsibility for that shift. The briefing also included the latest intelligence updates regarding criminality in the area. The number of police officers on each parade could vary enormously. On occasion, we would have less than half of the police numbers expected. Officers could be deployed elsewhere on demonstrations in central London, training courses, court appearances, sickness, and leave. This would result in the few that were left, shuttling from one call to another and handing over outstanding calls to the next shift. The chances of being able to patrol the streets on foot were rare. I don't think a lot has changed in that regard since. The parade was followed by an important event – a cup of tea in china cups with saucers.

The next day, I walked out of the police station in uniform on my own for the first time. I had no idea of the locality or exactly where I was. I popped into a local estate agent and 'borrowed' one of their folding maps of Barkingside. That way, I could find my way back to the station. One thing I noticed very soon was that people would not look me in the eye as I walked along.

Before I set off on my first foot patrol, I asked one of the older hands where would be a good place to concentrate my efforts. He gave me the name of a housing estate within walking distance. I set off to see what awaited me. The estate was one of those with a maze of footpaths and built in the 1960s. Small houses and even smaller flats were piled on top of each other. I felt sure that the architect did not live there. After about a hundred yards, a small bag of something soft and soggy was thrown at me but missed. It had been thrown from behind me and over a high fence. I continued my patrol. Shortly afterwards, I saw a middle-aged woman washing down her front door. She turned to me and said she was amazed and pleased to see a policeman on the street.

Farther on, I saw a teenager on a pushbike. He saw me and immediately pedalled off at speed down an alleyway while looking over his shoulder at me. Cycle theft was common in the area; I decided to catch him and investigate. At first, I began to gain on him, but soon he was travelling faster than I could run. I made a call on my radio, and a couple of police cars responded. The cyclist had now escaped. One of the police drivers told me it was always fun for the cyclists to goad a police officer into chasing them and that the bike was unlikely to be stolen. I then decided that a cup of tea would be in order.

One dark evening a couple of days later, I was on foot patrol, where I saw a car turn sharply and at speed into Horns Road from Eastern Avenue and accelerate towards me. In a second or two, I decided that this car might have been stolen. So far in my service, I hadn't stopped a car, and this was to be my first. I stood in the road with my torch flashing and held up my hand in the traditional method to indicate that it should stop. The car continued to accelerate, and I started to become a little worried. Suddenly, it veered away from me and passed close by. I managed to take a note of its rear number plate as it drove away. I recognised it as a Ford Capri. I wrote the number down on my estate agents' map. I tried to call the Barkingside Police Station control room, but there was a lot of chatter on the radio. I politely waited until the chatter ended and passed on my information. This was my first urgent call.

I was informed that a check on the police national computer (PNC) revealed it was a stolen car. A search by the police cars responding found it abandoned in a nearby street with the doors left wide open. It was brought to Barkingside Police Station for examination and parked in the station yard. I remember standing in the yard, gazing at my trophy and feeling quite pleased. The car was almost new and immaculate. A police cardboard label was attached to the door handle with my name on it. In the run of things, it didn't amount to much, but to me, I felt as though I had achieved something tangible and worthwhile without anyone's help. I had intercepted a group of reckless thieves and ensured that a stolen car was reunited with its no doubt grateful owner. This was what I had joined to do; to use my own initiative and ability to make the country just a bit safer.

I was impressed to find that these real police officers on my shift were decent human beings. They were not the monsters often portrayed by the media. They had a sense of humour and were not arrogant or pompous. Maybe I was lucky. Within my first week, I put my sergeant under extra pressure when he was already busy. I told him I had arrested a man for carrying an empty cardboard box in a public place and that his suspicious actions needed to be diligently investigated. I had in my hand a small empty box to add credibility. The look of horror on his face was priceless. Of course, I had made no such arrest. He took it well, I think.

The public does like to see a 'bobby on his beat'. It has been shown, however, that a PC walking along the street has little or no deterrent effect upon criminals. The sight of a policeman pacing the street certainly provides reassurance to the honest public, but it does little more than that. A police officer on foot cannot respond quickly to urgent calls. If fit, it would take him at least six minutes to run a mile. Burglars and muggers are not caught by police officers patrolling on foot. I consider that deploying a police officer on foot rather than in a car is a waste of time.

There was a definite pecking order in our police shift system. An inspector headed our shift. He, of course, was the 'headmaster' and respected. Our inspector was often described as a 'PC with pips' – pips referred to the rank markings on his shoulder. He had the ability to identify with and support his constables yet maintain authority. This was a tricky balance, but he succeeded. He was from a very wealthy family who had a famous business. He had a great sense of humour but would not tolerate insubordination or poor performance. He had worked his way up and knew all the tricks.

Our shift was blessed with excellent sergeants. There was a woman sergeant who was attractive and had a great personality. She was one of the better female police officers I was to encounter in my service. My supervising sergeant was the one who suffered my 'cardboard box' humour – he was responsible for assessing me. Another sergeant was famous for arresting everyone on a double-decker bus and bringing them all to the police station for questioning. He was an individual who knew the law and helped me on a number of occasions. Another sergeant, who was with us temporarily, had been a detective constable and was with us as part of his promotion to becoming a detective sergeant. He had a huge amount of experience regarding criminal investigation and was quite a character. He led me astray one afternoon by taking me for a pint or two while we were in full uniform. I didn't object. These were different times compared to today. He became a detective sergeant on the Flying Squad.

Next in the pecking order were the drivers of the fast-response Area Car. The Area Car was a high-powered SD1 Rover, and the driver had the top rating for driving skills. The concept of the Area Car was that it was to be free of routine tasks and be there to swiftly attend serious incidents. The Area Car was often assigned tasks directly from New Scotland Yard via the Scotland Yard radio channel. The call sign of our car was 'Juliette 5'. There was always a PC radio operator in the car to receive and record calls from the New Scotland Yard control centre. This PC would also provide a radio commentary via the New Scotland Yard channel to all North London Met mobile units should they be involved in a vehicle chase. These chases often crossed Divisional borders and could last for over ten minutes. The radio commentary would provide location, direction, and route and assist New Scotland Yard and other police units in tracking the chase.

This commentary is easier than it sounds, particularly when the adrenalin is flowing and the police car is being swung from side to side at high speed. The real hero, of course, was the driver. He had to balance speed with safety and yet not let the criminal escape. Often, there was no certainty as to what the occupants of the car being chased had done. They could have been armed with firearms having just robbed a bank, or they may have been fleeing because they had no insurance for their car. When the vehicle was eventually stopped, there was always the possibility of a violent confrontation. The armchair critics of police car chases always have the wonderful gift of hindsight.

The pecking order now moved down to the police van driver – traditionally a grizzled and cynical PC with about fifteen years or more of police service. It was he who decided on behalf of the shift if a new police policy was worthy or not. If not, it would be described as an 'L-O-B'. Translated, this means a load of b*******. The police van was usually used for transporting violent prisoners or for more than one prisoner. There was an outlandish and unsubstantiated rumour that it was sometimes used for Christmas shopping!

Further down the pecking list were the officers out of their two-year probationary period. They tended to think they knew it all but, of course, they did not. At the bottom of the list were officers such as me, who were probationers within their first two years of police service. We probationers probably comprised almost half the officers on the shift. We were keen, willing, and naive.

There was a tactic used by our shift for dealing with abusive yob gangs. Their behaviour was difficult to prosecute as they stopped their anti-social antics as soon as a police vehicle approached. The public was very reluctant to help, as they feared retribution. We knew exactly what they had been up to, but there was seldom any evidence to arrest them. There was one solution to this stalemate: we would order them into the back of the police van and drive off. The sight of this would, of course, please the residents.

We would then drive the yobs to Epping Forest, which was about five miles away, and remove the shoelaces from their trainers. The yobs would then be released and had to walk home without shoelaces. Their shuffling walk back home would take them over an hour, but it gave them time to reflect on their previous anti-social behaviour. To me, this was an example of practical policing that dealt with the problem and yet kept the kids out of the criminal justice system. We received no complaints regarding our actions. This police tactic would not be possible today as society would not approve. Or could I be wrong?

To the public, we were all highly experienced and knowledgeable because we wore the uniform. I was often asked for directions, and I almost always had to retrieve the (by now) grubby estate agents' map from my pocket to discuss route options. I was once running down a street in Chigwell, trying to catch a burglar who had been seen running from a nearby house. Suddenly, a motorist pulled alongside and shouted out to me for help. Distracted, I stopped and listened to him. I thought he might have been able to give me some information about the burglar. Instead, he told me he was lost and asked if I had a map. There I was, running fast, my police helmet tucked under my arm like a rugby ball, and he thought it was appropriate to stop me for directions? Did he think I was running for fun? I paused for a very deep and calming breath before helping him.

I was fortunate that I'd had a fair degree of life experience when I joined the police, and I think this was obvious to the police, criminals, and public. This certainly helped me through my probationary period. I recommend no one under twenty-one join the police. In America, twenty-one is the minimum age for a police recruit, and they retire at about forty-one.

It was a requirement for all recruits to be continually assessed by their sergeant and inspector regarding their aptitude for the demands of policing. Further assessment also took place at three monthly intervals at Bow Police Station, where I sat written exams and performed practical examinations. The training process was quite demanding, particularly when combined with the gruelling shift pattern. The probationary period lasted for two years.

An interesting incident occurred a few weeks after I joined Barkingside Police Station. I was patrolling on foot alone when I heard a burglar alarm activate nearby. I discovered it was a confectionary storage unit. It was a false alarm, and I waited for the owner to turn up to check the premises and turn it off. He did so, and, as a measure of his thanks to me, he gave me a large box of chocolates from the store. I took these back to the police station and suggested to my sergeant that we should share them out among our shift. He was horrified, saying that I must never do this as it was a 'gift' and amounted to corruption. Technically, I had crossed the line. Nothing further happened, and the chocolates were thrown in the bin. Was this a waste? Was it really corruption?

I discovered that police officers have a great deal of solidarity when one of them is in danger. About two weeks later, I was on the 'late-turn' shift. This shift ran from 3 pm to 11 pm. At about 9 pm, I was on foot patrol on my own in the vicinity of Gants Hill roundabout on Eastern Avenue. This was on the border with Ilford Police Station. The roundabout has Gants Hill Central Line tube station below and several connecting underground passageways.

As I walked by, I heard a lot of screaming and shouting from the station below. This could have been someone being attacked! As a precaution, I notified Barkingside Police Station by radio of my intention to go below ground and investigate. At that time, police radio transmissions could not be heard from below ground. I descended the steps, and as I walked along a tunnel, I heard a gang of rowdy youths making their way towards my location. I stood and waited until they turned a corner and abruptly faced me standing there. They were surprised to see me. Suddenly, they became well behaved and walked on. My job done, I walked back up the steps to the surface. As I did so, I saw police cars pulling up. They had responded at speed to my location in case I needed help.

Within a week or two, I arrested a rather unpleasant individual. He had been defacing public phone boxes by spraying anti-Semitic slogans. He had a can of spray paint and pro-Nazi literature in his pockets. He even had a Nazi identity card with his photograph in a Nazi uniform. I brought him back to Barkingside Police Station. I explained the facts of my arrest to the custody sergeant, who happened to be my reporting sergeant. The Nazi looked indignant and said, "What's wrong with being a Nazi? It's a free country." The custody sergeant gave half a smile and slowly shook his head. Oh, the irony. Special Branch showed an interest in the arrest, and I rather proudly sent them copies of all the arrest documentation.

On the evening of 10th April 1981, I was at home when there was a knock on the front door. I answered to a female police officer standing there. She told me that a riot had started in Brixton and that I was to report to my home police station as soon as possible.

I had no idea where Brixton was. I reported to Barkingside Police Station in a hurry, as it seemed urgent. Having arrived there, I was confronted with slow-motion chaos. Transport eventually arrived in the form of a traffic warden's green transit bus. By now, there were about ten of us ready to climb on board and head for this mystical place called Brixton.

There was not a lot of urgency, as several long-serving officers were not in search of action and were looking forward to imminent retirement. On the way to Brixton, we kept on getting lost, which surprised me at the time. I commandeered the A-Z map of London and guided us there. Now, I can see it was a delaying tactic to avoid the violent confrontation awaiting us.

Eventually, we were parked outside Brixton Police Station and remained there for over three hours. We could hear cries for help over the radio from police officers being attacked. The rumour was that three police officers had been killed during the riots. Judging by the apparent ferocity of the rioters, we assumed this rumour was accurate. I felt as though I had stepped into a war zone and facing a very uncertain future that night.

Meanwhile, we were ordered several times to leave our green traffic warden's van to consume bacon rolls and tea at the adjacent Brixton Police Station canteen. I'm still a fan of Met police bacon rolls, but six or seven could be seen as too much. During this time, police vans would return from the riots with injured officers while we were kept on standby waiting for deployment. On occasion, I saw police vans with bandaged officers being deployed from Brixton Police Station to again attend the riots. It was all rather surreal and frustrating being sat in our van with nothing to do.

Alarms sounded from the many looted shops nearby, and the air was full of the smell of burning buildings and cars. I had no idea why we had to remain in place, doing nothing but eat bacon rolls and listen to the many police distress calls on the radio.

At about 2 am, we received a radio call to deploy on foot from our van to Stockwell Road, which was opposite Brixton Police Station. We were not given a reason for doing this, and I thought it was simply some sort of administrative task. We assumed we were in a backwater and quite some distance from the rioting. We walked from our van as a group and saw a crowd of about two hundred rioters in Stockwell Road approaching the police station. In hindsight, we had obviously been held back in reserve in case of such a situation as this. The crowd was shouting at us; they were obviously in high spirits and had probably been rioting all evening. All the police officers with me decided to form a line across Stockwell Road to try to hold them back. We amounted to about a dozen officers. Should we have retreated to Brixton Police Station when confronted with these odds? In retrospect, after all these years, I think we should have. Today, such a small number of unprotected officers would never have been allowed to confront such a large crowd of aggressive rioters.

The crowd was now moving purposefully towards us. I felt that this was not going to end well for us, but at the same time, I didn't feel too scared. In my mind, we were all that was available to protect not only Brixton Police Station from destruction but also the peaceful people of Brixton and the rest of London from a riotous, violent, and swelling mob. We were now literally the thin blue line. We had no protective clothing or riot shields. As a recruit, I had had no training for this sort of event. Of note, there was an extra strap to our police helmets at that time which we could use during a riot. This strap was all we had in our armoury, and I don't think the rioters were deterred by this very minor addition to our safety.

There was a pause as the rioters approached.

Objects were thrown at us. A police officer somewhere to my left shouted, "Clear the streets!" It almost sounded like, "Fix bayonets!" I had no idea what 'clearing the streets' involved or meant, but, as one, all the other officers drew their wooden truncheons and held them vertically in front of themselves at arm's length. I did the same. Nothing was said between us. This was a very new situation to me; just a few months before, I had been a member of the public.

We all started to slowly walk forwards towards the large crowd. This was not instinctive. No officer said that we should advance, but it seemed the right thing to do. We were there to protect the public, after all. After about ten yards, we, as one, broke into a run towards the rioters. We were in a London location unknown to us, vastly outnumbered and unarmed, advancing at a run towards a large crowd that, to our knowledge, had recently murdered three police officers. I was absolutely amazed to see that all the rioters suddenly took fright. Their faces were no longer full of arrogance; they now looked scared. They stopped, turned, and ran away in all directions to avoid us.

My blood was up by then, and, with another officer, I chased a group of four rioters down a side alley named Astoria Walk to the right-hand side of the road. After running about two hundred yards after them, we decided to retreat, as we were now on our own and without a radio to call for backup. It was a wise decision. We then returned to our van outside Brixton Police Station.

I was very impressed with the leadership shown by an unknown police constable calling upon us to 'clear the streets'. I was also impressed by the response of all the officers to this command. Our cohesive response had not only stopped the rioters but had also dispersed them. We made no arrests, but that was not important. We had turned the balance in our favour at street level and without the need for direction from senior officers, who were not there anyway. I then realised that police constable leaders at street level had a crucial role to play in policing. These street-level leaders were never recognised or appreciated by those police officers who held high rank. Their high ranks were matched by equally high salaries and pensions.

I have spoken to a few police officers about this incident over the years. In their view, that was the way to deal with rioters. Today, we have a game of Aunt Sally between the rioters and police: the rioters throw missiles at the police, and the police hide behind their riot shields and body armour. If the police try to move forward, they are severely hampered by the weight of their equipment, and the rioters know this. Stalemate in effect.

We were not needed again that night, and perhaps our brave and reckless actions had, in some way, helped diminish the riot. At dawn, we headed back to Barkingside Police Station and home. A few of us had fallen asleep in our seats by now. I took all this in my stride as part of being a new police officer. But, without orders or direction from anyone, we had taken back control of the streets.

One memory remained with me: rioters enjoyed rioting. It was seen as fun to throw objects at the police and, as a bonus, have the chance to window shop with a brick and 'own' free electrical devices of your choice.

The best cure for a riot is rain. Nobody riots in rain. In fact, crime falls drastically on a wet day. Criminals don't like getting wet. Perhaps sprinklers would be more effective than noisy burglar alarms?

I was to return to Brixton on several occasions in the coming days just to provide extra policing. This involved a lot of waiting about in case there was another riot. On one occasion during this period, I was off duty and went to a party in Brixton in with four of my friends from the Royal Navy. There were also dozens of university students present. As I walked up the path to the front door, several students held up dust bin lids towards me as a form of mock salute. (Dust bin lids had been used by police officers during the riot as improvised shields). I felt slightly uncomfortable among the sixty or so people there. There was some mild sarcasm directed at me; they were all aware of my job. I didn't stay there for too long.

Burglary was a very real problem for the people of Barkingside. Sometimes, there would be up to eighteen houses a day broken into while the occupants were away at work. This was distressful to the owners and took up a lot of police time, both in reporting and investigating. Few burglars were caught. One day, I got lucky. There was a report from a member of the public that a man had been seen leaving a house with a black bin liner full of stolen property. He was seen getting on a bus. I was nearby and stopped the bus. The burglar was sitting on the top deck with his incriminating swag bag full of silver ornaments on his knee. He freely admitted to me his involvement in the burglary. I bought him a cup of tea back at the station. He was then handed over to the CID for further investigation (the CID handled all burglary investigations).

About two hours later, I received a message that the burglar wanted to see me. I met him in the custody suite. He apparently didn't want to speak with the CID anymore and had somehow fallen out with them. I interviewed him, and he admitted burglaries he had committed in Barkingside recently. He also admitted to burglaries in his hometown of Hackney. This was all down to the tea I had bought him! I don't think I won any CID allies because of this.

Attending football matches was something I did not enjoy. I was rarely posted inside the football ground with a chance to see the game – that perk was usually reserved for police officers local to that ground. One of the exceptions was West Ham, where I often stood among the home supporters on the terraces. (Seating was not compulsory at that time). The atmosphere provided by the West Ham fans was electric. I remember applauding a tremendous goal. For a moment, I forgot what I was. I received a dozen pats on the back. Well, I think they were pats! I did enjoy the local Leyton Orient home matches. There was a great atmosphere, and we were usually within the football ground. The police hut always had a brew of tea on the go.

I was never one for harassing motorists. However, I found one aspect of this to be worthwhile: bus lanes! As a motorist myself, I hated queuing in traffic and someone would cut in using the bus lane and jump to the head of the queue. So, I would apply justice to bus lanes when next on duty. I regularly found that many motorists engaging in bus-lane offending had a criminal lifestyle. I kept those motorists who were just being foolish stationary long enough to remove any progress they thought they might have made. I would then give them a warning. The motorists in the queue often gave me a 'thumbs up' sign!

One motorist was not too happy at my request to pull over. As he stepped out of his car, I noticed he was about 6 feet 9 inches tall. He wore a Stetson hat and cowboy boots. He grabbed me by my coat lapels, and my police helmet fell to the ground. He said no one was going to send him back to prison! He threatened to run me down if I used my radio to call for help. He then walked back to his car. I requested assistance on my radio as he speedily reversed up the bus lane. By chance, there was a police car farther up the road, and they received my message. They chased his car down a side street and brought him into the police station. It turned out that he had never been to prison or even been arrested before. He was taking his mother's cat to the vet, and he said his behaviour was caused by stress. Two of the motorists waiting in the queue volunteered to attend court and support my account. The culprit received a small fine. The local paper had a headline that read, 'Rhinestone Cowboy Rides Roughshod Over the Boys In Blue', with a full-length picture of him in his cowboy outfit.

There was a shortage of police officers, even back then, and I give the following as an example. I had just finished work for the day and was about to leave for home. As I was passing the control room, I heard a radio call for any police unit to respond to a report of men stealing from a car. There was no response, as all officers were dealing with arrests or other calls. I paused and considered my options. I put my head around the control room door and informed them that I would attend. I was not qualified to drive a police car at this stage as I was in my probationary period, so my only option was to use my own car. I saw another officer from my shift, and he agreed to join me. By now, I had booked out a police radio.

I drove about two miles to the location and saw the thieves driving off in their van. I pulled up in front of them at a junction, and they stopped. They were surprised to see two police officers in uniform step out of a very much non-police car. As we spoke to them for a couple of minutes, police cars arrived with blue lights to save the day. The van was full of stolen wheels and other parts. All four were convicted of many thefts. The volume of paperwork involved in the investigation was a shock to me. They had admitted many offences, and the paperwork was multiplied by four, as all four were jointly involved. The CID had taken on the case due to its complexity, but it was all handed back to me as the CID was, allegedly, too busy at that time. The reality was that I had upset a detective constable by obtaining confessions from one of the criminals. This had been too much, and had upset his ego.

There was no CPS at this time, and I often appeared at the magistrate's court as a prosecutor on my own for criminal offences such as use of an offensive weapon, theft, and assault. Of course, the accused would be represented by a solicitor. I didn't lose a single prosecution. I would borrow some dusty law books from the CID office and take them with me to court. I would place them on my table in front of the magistrates and next to the defending solicitor. I made sure that my pile of books was bigger than his. On several occasions when addressing the magistrate, the defence solicitor referred to me as his "learned friend". A 'learned friend' is a fellow lawyer.

There was also a constant demand for officers to attend demonstrations. The public perception of demonstrations was that each one was a riot. Not so. The vast majority were tedious affairs that amounted to me arriving exceedingly early to the event. I would receive what was known as 'force feeding' at a public building nearby, such as a school. The breakfast always comprised bacon, eggs, and beans on a paper plate with a bread roll, butter, and marmalade. Following this, I would stand in one place for many hours until the event was over. Dull it certainly was. The only benefit was overtime payments; it was impossible to accomplish this lengthy deployment within an eight-hour shift. The overtime was useful as it helped supplement my inadequate income to support my family.

In May 1981, I attended a demonstration in central London along with a colleague from my shift. It was late in the evening, and we were expected to patrol on foot back and forth along Whitehall near Trafalgar Square. The streets were almost empty, and all was quiet, with more police officers than the public. I suggested to my colleague that we do some exploring, as we obviously had no policing value there. We walked across Trafalgar Square and ended up in Soho. Compared to residential Barkingside, the place was alive with activity and bright lights. I noticed that the hot-dog sellers ran away when we approached. Of course, they were illegal and not licensed. You had to be crazy to eat anything they sold. I felt we were of more use here than in deserted Trafalgar Square.

Suddenly, a car pulled up alongside, and out stepped a very irate uniform inspector. He stared at us and said, "Where the hell are you two from?" Before I could speak, he looked at our shoulder numbers and said, "J District. Where's that?" I explained we were on a demonstration near Trafalgar Square and had decided to move on as it was all quiet back there. I thought he would have appreciated our help by being in his section. It was equivalent in his eyes to leaving our post without authority. When we returned to Trafalgar Square, the inspector in charge also tore into us and said he was considering using the discipline code against us. This could have cost us a fine or possible dismissal. It was as if we were deserters. I was not aware of these restrictions and was just being proactive in seeking out criminality. That was my job, after all. But it seemed that such rigid thinking was detrimental to efficient policing. I was to meet this attitude repeatedly during my police service.

Barkingside had several commuter car parks next to London Underground stations. Of course, thieves knew that the owners would be away for most of the day at work. There were almost daily thefts – not only of cars but also parts. The stolen cars were often used in crime. I used to carry out covert observations on these car parks when the opportunity arose. I couldn't commit more than a couple of hours at a time, but the results were always worth the effort. I would find a vantage point overlooking the car park and equip myself with a pair of binoculars, a police radio, and my notebook. It was rather like fishing and waiting for a bite. By this method, I often spoilt the day for thieves when I caught them red-handed. All that was required was a call on my radio to summon help.

An incident occurred that I found distasteful, but I had little option but to comply. One evening, I was on foot patrol on my own near Gants Hill tube station. There was a drinking bar nearby, known to be frequented by active criminals. Parked outside this bar was a Rolls Royce with no tax disc. Why would someone who could afford to run a Rolls Royce have no tax disc? I drove a third-hand car, but I paid for my road tax. I walked around the car, examining it, then began to write an official report form regarding the 'no road tax' offence.

The bar had a glass frontage, and I had obviously been seen. A serving detective constable from Barkingside CID approached me from the bar in a slightly agitated state. He told me that the owner of the Rolls Royce was in the bar with him and was providing valuable information to him regarding the criminal activity of others. The detective told me that if I reported his car for 'no tax', this flow of information would cease. I didn't believe this detective – I suspected some other motive for this request. However, I was concerned that, if he was telling the truth, I didn't want to be obstructive and petty when more important issues were at stake. I paused for a moment or two and told the detective that the Rolls Royce needed to be road taxed as soon as possible. The detective was delighted with this compromise and returned to the bar. Some years later, this detective would be imprisoned for corruption.

There were risks to my life on occasion. One such time was when I drove with a sergeant to a council tower bock in Hackney one evening. We needed to interview a resident there. We walked along the paved path approaching the communal door. When we were a few feet away, a large potted plant crashed to the ground next to me and shattered into hundreds of pieces. It had been dropped from many floors up. We looked up but could see nothing. It would have killed either of us had the drop been slightly more accurate. Luck was on my side that evening. I was very wary after that when approaching tower blocks.

There are despicable criminals who prey on

the elderly with various scams. One tactic was to knock on the door of an elderly resident and suggest their chimney needed re-pointing, offering to carry out the work for what would transpire to be an excessive fee. The resident would be enticed to accept the offer by being convinced that the criminal was qualified, experienced, and well-meaning.

While on an urgent call elsewhere, I passed a builder's van outside an elderly resident's bungalow. The builder was at the front door speaking to him. I noted the number plate on the van as I passed. I returned to the house about an hour later. The builder had carried out a tiny amount of re-pointing of the lowest standard possible! He must have used a shovel to apply it. He charged £600 for about ten minutes of 'work'. This was in 1982. Today, that would be about £3,000 in value. The resident was very unhappy with the price charged and the standard of work. He felt he had been intimidated into paying. I couldn't immediately trace the van. However, about a week later, I saw the same van and stopped it. I arrested the driver for deception. However, the court rejected the case. They decided that it was not a criminal matter and should have been dealt with by a solicitor as a work quality issue. I tried my best!

At about this time, I was on a day off and had

arranged to take my seven-year-old son to see the film *Raiders of the Lost Ark* at Barkingside cinema. I had parked my car nearby and was taking a shortcut through an alleyway at the rear of the high street shops. As is usual with most high street shops, residential flats were situated above them, with stairways at the rear. As I walked through the alleyway with my son, I noticed two men pushing at the door of a flat on the first floor, trying to use their body weight to force it open. One of the men tried to open one of the windows. This was an attempted burglary.

Rather than confront them myself and risk being assaulted and losing them in the crowds, I continued to the end of the alleyway and went into the nearest shop. I told the staff that I was an off-duty police officer and asked if I could use their phone. Barkingside Police Station was about six hundred yards away, and my own shift was on duty. I explained the situation, describing the two men and where I had last seen them a few seconds ago.

I waited outside the shop for the first police car to arrive. When it did, I sat inside with my son, and we started to look for the burglars. I spotted them walking along the next alleyway, obviously looking for flats to burgle. More officers attended at the same time, and a chase on foot started along the alleyways. I joined in, carrying my son. Both burglars ran into a snooker hall. The officers entered, but the burglars could not be seen. The snooker games were being played as normal. However, a careful search under the tables found both burglars hidden away.

Both were arrested and led to police cars. One was placed into the rear of a police car near me by a uniform sergeant. The sergeant turned to me as he closed the car door and said, with a big smile on his face, that I had done well. Unseen by the sergeant, the burglar now opened the car door on the opposite side and ran off. The chase began again! Fortunately, he was caught by an officer a few hundred yards away.

I took my son home. We missed the film; he was, of course, disappointed. I spent the next few hours back at the police station, writing my pocketbook notes and preparing a written statement. Both burglars were later charged with attempted burglary of the flat and were found guilty in court.

Chigwell was part of Barkingside and made famous by the comedy series *Birds of a Feather*. It was typified by houses built in ostentatious splendour adorned with splendid Greek pillars and stone lions. A number of these houses were owned by the criminal fraternity, who had done well out of a career of crime. Several had been part of the Krays gang back in the 1960s. I went to one such address as a covert alarm had sounded and alerted the police. There was a Rolls Royce on the drive without a tax disc. I was met at the door by a man wearing tracksuit bottoms, a string vest, and a range of tattoos. He was the owner of what would now be a house worth several million pounds. Not what I had expected!

So, in the space of a short time, I had confronted not only rioters but also the unfounded allegation of acquiring, corruptly, a large box of chocolates.

There was an expression called GTP – 'Good to Police'. Some organisations were GTP. Cinemas would provide free entry to police officers. We never had to pay for a kebab at the take-away outlets. Some retail outlets also provided discounts. It seemed perfectly normal to us at the time, but this practice has now died out. Was it a form of corruption?

There were so many varied incidents to deal with during my two-year probationary period, and it is not possible to list them all here.

I would like to add that, at this time, the CID was rather 'traditional'. Many female police officers were reluctant to enter the CID office, as the banter would be regarded today as extremely sexist and intimidating. Other female police officers could certainly return the banter and perhaps enjoy the sparring. Female police officers were known as 'Plonks' – 'Persons of Little or No Knowledge'.

Friday afternoon was always when the CID had an end of week drink, with scotch being top of the menu. There was some resentment from the uniform officers towards the CID, whom they saw as having a much easier life. The CID work shift was mainly 9–5, with occasional evening and weekend duties. There was only ever one detective on night duty, and his role was to provide advice to uniform officers regarding serious and complex crime. A detective constable had the same rank as a police constable, but in many ways, the detective had greater status and more varied career prospects. There was also quite a lengthy selection process to become a detective, which I think created a feeling of elitism among the CID. An errant detective could also be returned to uniform as a punishment but never the other way around. I think this rankled with many uniform officers. There certainly were CID officers who were 'flash' and arrogant. There was always a suggestion of corruption in the air, but this was very rarely proved.

Towards the end of my probationary period,

I was posted to what was known as the 'Beat Crimes Unit' for a month. The unit was composed of about eight uniform constables in plain clothes with a sergeant supervisor. Our role was to investigate minor crimes such as vandalism and minor assaults. My month there was to gain further experience as a police officer. I would be allocated about five crimes a day to investigate. For most crimes, there was little chance of catching the offender, and many were probably reported for insurance purposes.

What it did teach me, though, was that even minor crimes can take up a disproportionate amount of police time. When I had the chance, I would set myself up near a tube station car park and wait for thieves to strike. I made arrests this way. Some said I was lucky; my attitude was that you make your own luck. The detective chief inspector was critical of my overtime claim for the month, which was more than anyone on Beat Crimes or the CID. However, my arrest figures were explained, and his attitude then changed for the better. Throughout my police service, I found that senior management was critical of officers who earned more overtime than average. They saw it as an abuse of resources. Quite the opposite was true: high overtime earners always had a high arrest rate. Not just in quantity but also in quality. I never found women to have high arrest rates – they didn't seem as interested as men.

Having completed my probationary period, I was nominated for a driving course. This course would allow me to drive a standard police car but did not allow me to engage in pursuits. Training was about four weeks long and based at Hendon, although we took long, high-speed drives – not only in London but also out in Essex and Hertfordshire. My instructor was a retired police officer who had flown RAF Hurricane fighters during World War Two. The Hurricane was a similar aircraft to the Spitfire. He told me that driving a car safely was far more challenging than flying a Hurricane.

I passed my driving course but had only driven a police car for a few weeks before I broke an unwritten rule. My humour caught up with me, and I found myself posted elsewhere.

I began to realise that joining the Met had perhaps not been such a good idea. Had I joined a police force other than London, my income would have gone a lot further. I had been accepted by Greater Manchester Police but turned it down in favour of the Royal Navy. Semi-detached houses in Greater Manchester were far less than half the price compared to London. Also, commuting times would have been a lot shorter and therefore cheaper.

I was posted to what was sometimes referred to as a 'riot van'. Its technical term was the DSU or District Support Unit. This was early 1983, and riots had taken place in Toxteth, Brixton, and in other UK cities. I received the training I needed at a riot school in West London, where mock streets, shops, and houses were constructed for this purpose. Hidden behind our long shields and helmets, we were battered daily with lobbed wooden bricks. I reflected upon my experience almost two years earlier in Brixton, when we had no protection, but we had the speed and agility to charge and disperse the rioters.

The morale of the crew in our unit was high. It was one of those vans with a large grill to protect the windscreen. We bonded well, and the banter was marvellous. We had an Asian PC on our unit – I think he was from Ceylon. He was a vegetarian, which was unusual in those days. When we had meat feast pizzas, he'd be asked if he'd prefer perhaps a lettuce-flambe. He accepted it all as good fun and would give as good as he got. Today, due to political correctness, no such banter would ever happen. When I next met him some years later, he had achieved the rank of chief inspector.

Although we fortunately did not have to attend a riot, we did, on one occasion, end up in potentially serious trouble. It was at about midnight on a Friday night, and we were slowly meandering along Ilford high street. A large group of youths was gathered, and, without any warning, they started fighting among themselves. The eight of us climbed out of the van to break it up, but this didn't work out too well. They all turned on us, and we were forced to back up to the van and fend them off. Fortunately, our driver had the presence of mind to radio for help as we neared the fight. Help arrived with much noise and blue lights. Wonderful to see and hear! Now it was our turn. We each made an arrest. We tried to sit them on the seats in the van, but they still struggled with us. It must have been the alcohol they had consumed kicking in or perhaps other 'substances'. There were a few bruises between us but nothing serious. They were all charged with public disorder offences and admitted their guilt in court.

I had found my life as a uniform police constable frustrating. I was deluged with commitments that took me away from the policing I had joined for. I just wanted to catch the criminals. Answering phones, dealing with lost dogs, escorting prisoners, and reporting road traffic collisions at the front desk were not what I had joined for. I had been given a respite on the 'riot van', but it wasn't a permanent solution. I therefore applied for the CID. This was perhaps not a wise decision in retrospect.

CID Training Crime Squad 1983-85

My application for the CID required that I apply for the crime squad. The crime squad was composed of about thirty uniform police officers who wanted to be selected for the CID. To be selected, they were required to exhibit high arrest rates and work in plain clothes for about two years.

My application was successful, and in May 1983, I started plain clothes duties at Wanstead Police Station. Our remit was the whole of 'J' District in East London. This district included Leyton, Leytonstone, Ilford, Wanstead, Walthamstow, Barkingside, Chingford, Woodford, and Loughton. We were in an annex adjacent to Wanstead Police Station.

This was all quite an abrupt change for me. I felt a lot of loyalty towards my uniform colleagues who, in some way, I think regarded me as something of a traitor in selecting the CID option. The crime squad unit was composed of a detective inspector in charge overall, with three detective sergeants to assist him. There were two detective constables to provide guidance for us, as well as four uniform officers temporarily working in plainclothes with many years' policing experience. They were known as 'Parent Constables'.

I felt somewhat lost in this new environment, and I initially decided that I would stay with the crime squad for six months, just so that I could say I had done it for the sake of experience. My previous uniform life had been one of routine work, with little opportunity to seek out criminals. Now, the opposite was true. I had all the time in the day to find and arrest criminals. But where were they?

In some ways, I now had the role of a hunter. I quickly decided that the best way to make arrests was to take a plain car from the limited pool of vehicles we had available and patrol the crime-prevalent areas of Leyton and Leytonstone. I was now partnered with a PC who had the same attitude as me. He had been a PC at Leyton Police Station and was as keen as I. He had a degree in something or other but, more importantly, he had a common-sense approach to policing and a sense of humour. Our favourite vehicle was a canary yellow Austin Metro. Its looks didn't strike fear into the criminal fraternity, but it certainly didn't look like a police car.

Unknown to me at the time, two officers there were extremely corrupt. I only discovered this years later. They were excellent police officers, and I trusted them both at the time. Both were intelligent, very capable, and articulate. I learned a lot from them. They both had leadership qualities that were missing in so many senior ranks.

I have a theory that CID officers become corrupt because they believe that they are not financially appreciated by the system. The police do not financially reward performance: police officers are paid according to their rank. CID officers can also often have unsupervised access to substantial quantities of seized cash from criminals. Additionally, CID officers often have close contact with criminals, particularly when the criminal is an informant providing information and seeks favours in return.

It's a little-known fact that most police officers are not interested in promotion. When I say most, I would say about 85% think this way. This 85% despise most senior officers for having escaped the front line, as they were not capable of doing the job of a PC in the first place. As a former military officer, I have to say that the selection process for promotion in the police is bizarre. My selection as a military officer was very thorough. For the police, it amounts to a written application, which is always supported by supervisors as it is too much trouble to turn it down. The next stage is an interview, where the applicant is anonymous to the selectors. The selectors have no idea of their ability or background. The applicant is asked questions such as their performance regarding the availability of crèches for staff. Tick-box answers are sought. Based upon this thirty-minute interview, police managers are created. Managers are not leaders; they enforce policy. Leaders have a habit of leading. The police need leaders.

I eventually found that the crime squad suited me. It took me perhaps three months or more to find my feet and adjust to the different pace of life.

I became successful with both the quantity and quality of my arrests. I was not interested in what was known as 'perchers'. Perchers were easy arrests, such as arresting someone at their home address on a warrant for not appearing at court.

My first arrest of a drug dealer occurred through slightly unusual circumstances. I met an informant willing to provide information about a drug dealer's address. This informant had been rejected by other officers as being potentially unreliable. After a conversation with him, I decided to act upon what he said. He was not a typical 'junkie' and was from a professional background. To verify this information, I and a few colleagues kept observation on the dealer's home address. We were in a plain vehicle parked about one hundred yards away. After about half an hour, as predicted by my informant, the dealer drove off. He was about twenty years old. I managed to follow him for about a mile. Surveillance normally requires many vehicles, but I was successful on this occasion so far. We watched him visit two addresses for several minutes each.

I was granted search warrants the next day from a magistrate for all three addresses. These were my first search warrants ever. All the addresses were expensive properties in well-to-do areas. There had never been any criminality at the home address of the suspected dealer or the other addresses. Should I launch searches on these addresses? Could it all be a massive mistake and seized upon by the media to my detriment of myself and the Met Police? I had to decide.

I decided to search all three addresses. I did not seek advice from superior officers – there was no need in my mind to do so. I selected officers for the searches and, fortunately as it turned out, I requested the help of a drugs search dog and handler for the search of the dealer's home address.

I organised that we should search the addresses at 6 am the following morning. I didn't sleep too well as there was obviously a lot of doubt on my mind.

First, we went to the dealer's address. I knocked on the door, and an older woman answered, who I later discovered was his mother. She was naked. She screamed when she realised that I was the police and had a search warrant. She wrapped herself in a towel that she had been carrying and ran upstairs, screaming. The property was a maisonette and on several floors. I began to feel that this was all a dreadful mistake and would, without doubt, make the Sunday papers as another example of Met Police incompetence.

I then walked through the door and up the stairs. There was absolute chaos in the house. The drugs dog behind me indicated something in an alcove. The mother then ran past me naked into the garden at the rear. She hid a bag of drugs in some bushes within the back garden. The drugs dog spotted that.

To sum up, a large number of drugs were seized, plus a substantial sum of money. The drugs were cocaine and large cannabis resin blocks. The other two addresses had cannabis resin that had physical matches with the cannabis seized at the dealer's address. Mother and son were arrested and convicted of possessing a very substantial quantity of controlled drugs. The occupants of the other two addresses were also convicted.

Both were taken to Ilford Police Station. Our detective inspector then arrived. I think he understood my thoughts. He proclaimed while looking at me, "He who dares, wins". There was truth in that. I slept soundly that night.

I realised that I was now entering a different arena to my past life in the police. My responsibilities for those drug searches were way beyond my previous uniform self.

The informant who had provided me with the information to obtain these arrests again contacted me regarding drug dealers in other parts of North London. I passed this information on, and it turned out to be accurate. However, it cost me money paying him for the information, and I could not claim it back from the police who, at that time, required a conviction before releasing payment. But conviction could take more than a year. It was far too late for my purposes. Technically, paying a member of the public from my own pocket for information could have got me sacked. However, there were vast savings to the public purse by using an informant.

During this time with the crime squad, I was involved with my police partner in trying to establish the address of a major drug dealer in an East London tower block. We parked nearby and kept observation. After about an hour, a car pulled up, and the driver went into the tower block. Nothing unusual in that. But, about five minutes later, he returned to his car. We followed him, and once he was away from the tower block, we pulled him over. We searched him, and he had a wrap of cocaine in his jacket. We told him that if he said where he had bought the drug, we would drop the cocaine down the drain, and he would not be arrested. He told us the exact address and watched us drop the drug down the drain. His information was correct. A drug dealer was therefore arrested, and a range of drugs seized. Was our action ethical? In my view, yes, it was. Was it legal? No.

Not long after this, a large police operation was launched against drug dealers in this estate. The doors on each of the drug dealer's flats were reinforced to protect not just against police forced entry but also forced entry from rival drug dealers' intent on stealing money and drugs. For the police to force open these doors by conventional means would have taken time. During this time, the dealer would flush the drugs down the toilet, thereby eliminating vital evidence.

Someone came up with the idea of using chainsaws to cut our way quickly through the doors. What could possibly go wrong? The plan was that trained council employees with chainsaws would join police search and arrest teams at each address. At 6 am, the chain saws would be started outside each door. The door would be cut down in a few seconds, and the police officers armed with a search warrant would enter and search the premises. But this did not go to plan.

At the first address, the chainsaw wouldn't start. As the operator repeatedly and noisily pulled on the starter cord, the drug dealer opened the door and said, "Can I be of help, officers?" At the next address, the chainsaw started readily enough, but it immediately jammed in the door, and the operator couldn't move it. After a few seconds, the drug dealer opened the door and said, "Is there anything I can help you officers with?" On the way to the next address, the officers and the chain-saw operator became stuck in the narrow lift when the winding mechanism failed. After a minute or so, the operator became very agitated and screamed that he suffered from extreme claustrophobia and wanted to fire up the chainsaw and slice his way out. This was concerning to the officers.

This was not a successful police operation, and the chainsaw method was not repeated.

A few months later, I was involved with other officers in the search of a drug dealer's home. There was an extensive amount of Class A drugs found with the help of a search dog. All this took some time. During this time, clients repeatedly attended the address to buy drugs. Visits became so frequent that we had to ask for a marked police car to be parked outside to deter these buyers. But no, they continued to attend the address. One caller asked me where else he could go now that his supplier had been arrested! We could, of course, have arrested these callers, as they were breaking the law trying to buy controlled drugs. But it was not a practical option – we had more than enough to do anyway.

On Church Road, Leytonstone, there used to be a shop selling military medals and books. In late 1984, I received information from the owner that a couple of men had been in his shop offering to sell a large bag of military medals in a plastic bag. He told them it would take some time to value these medals and asked if they could return the following day, when he would be able to give them an accurate estimate. He suspected the medals were stolen, and after they left his shop, he informed the police. My crime partner and I visited him and took a written statement to confirm details and their descriptions. We confirmed through research that the medals had been stolen in a local burglary. He had a small office to one side of the counter, and we waited there the next day in case the thieves returned.

After about a two-hour wait, both men came into the shop. They were both six feet tall, aged in their twenties and well built; they certainly didn't look like the average medal collector. They asked the shop owner about the medals. At this point, we emerged from our hiding place and announced who we were. We explained why they were being arrested and tried to lead them to our car nearby. When outside the shop, they started to struggle with us. Both were very strong. I made a radio call for help but was told there were no police units available. I was beginning to worry, but just at that moment, a police van came around the corner. I waved, and it stopped – now there were another two officers on the scene. Not surprisingly, the struggle died away, and we were able to handcuff them. Due to their criminal history, both received prison sentences, and the medals were returned to a delighted owner.

I hated paperwork. Today, paper has largely disappeared to be replaced by a keyboard. This has not reduced the amount of time an officer spends on administrative work, however. If anything, digital systems have increased the amount of time an officer has to be away from his primary role of keeping the public safe. In my opinion, the advancement of digital technology has reduced police numbers on the street by 20%. Digital inputs such as reporting a crime are now lengthy and excessively supervised by teams permanently behind desks. These teams will reject many reports for further work by the officer. This applies to all police activity. Over twenty years ago, Tony Blair created a morass of controlling regulations that impeded the police in their operational work. Police initiative has become stifled and encourages the officer to do as little as possible.

I so despised paperwork and being tied to a desk that I would take a typewriter to the police car and type away in the back seat as we kept watch, for example, on a car park. I was doing this one day after an arrest earlier that morning. We were keeping observation on a car park in Leyton that thieves were very fond of stealing from. After about half an hour, my colleague saw two youths enter the car park. He recognised them as local car thieves. We saw them trying a few car door handles to see if they were open. Suddenly, they opened the door of one of the cars and jumped inside. Within a couple of seconds, they had the engine started. By now, we were running across the car park to catch them. Too late! The car started to move. I instinctively grabbed the driver's door handle. For a couple of moments, I thought that I was Superman and with my secret powers be able to hold the car back... Not so, of course. The car sped off and left us standing in a cloud of dust. But all was not lost: my colleague had recognised them, and later, we paid them a visit at home. They were shocked to know they had been recognised. Both appeared at court and were found guilty of stealing the car.

My knowledge of cockney rhyming slang was poor. One afternoon, I was speaking to a burglar in his cell. He asked me for his 'almonds'. I could not understand his request. My colleague was one of the few Met officers who were from London. He started laughing at my predicament. 'Almonds' is rhyming slang for almond rocks – as in socks.

Ever had your bicycle stolen? This example of blatant theft will surprise you. Once again, I was with my colleague, sat in a car watching a commuter car park on the lookout for thieves. We were parked outside Newbury Park tube station in Ilford and could see anyone who walked into the adjacent commuter car park. I had a newspaper and, for amusement, I had cut two eye holes so that I could view goings-on without arousing suspicion. I had just done that when a large transit van pulled up near us. Three men stepped out, each carrying a pair of bolt cutters. There was a large cycle rack nearby where commuters left their bikes chained up in the hope that they'd still be there when they returned. Systematically, these three men cut the locks off all the bikes in just a few seconds. My suspicions were aroused! These three men were well built, to say the least. I called for backup on the radio. The bikes were loaded onto the van. Nobody else nearby seemed to spot this outlandish theft.

The van drove onto Eastern Avenue, heading east. We drove some distance behind. I kept up a commentary on the radio so that police vehicles would know where it was. A few minutes later, a police car with its blue lights on overtook us and stopped the van. All three were arrested and convicted of theft. All the bikes were returned to their owners. Whether they parked their bikes there again or not, I never found out.

Police corruption now appeared for the first time in my police service, but this would not be the last time. A 'parent PC' was with us on the crime squad to guide us with the benefit of his experience. He liked a bet, and he offered us all a financial share in his newly bought greyhound. I had a certificate from him to prove it. I think my share cost about £10. The dog was not particularly successful and tended to be last. But, one day, this 'parent PC' was arrested: he had been demanding money from motorists at home who possessed forged MOT certificates. He threatened to arrest and charge them if they did not pay up. He was successful in his criminal enterprise: every motorist he approached paid him off. But there was one exception: a young motorist paid him and then told his father about it all. His indignant father immediately rang the police. The corrupt parent PC was arrested and suspended. Word spread rapidly, and we destroyed our greyhound certificates as we all felt tainted with his criminal behaviour. The parent PC was later imprisoned. We never did find out what happened to the greyhound!

It was a shock to all of us. I later learned that there was no typical profile for a corrupt officer. I also learned that police corruption takes many forms and is not always confined to an officer acting alone. Sir Robert Mark, the Metropolitan police commissioner, had not been entirely successful in eradicating corruption.

Had I experienced any police brutality? No. This was a surprise to me as so much was made of this in the media. I had certainly experienced brutality toward the police. This was not to say that police brutality did not exist, but my experiences to date suggested that it was rare.

I found that this proactive style of policing suited me. I was independent, free to follow my instincts, and the master of my destiny. I was also successful. But this freedom could not last forever. After about eighteen months on the crime squad, the day approached when I had to sit on a selection board for the post as a detective constable. By now, I had passed the sergeant's examination to a high standard and was expected to soon return to uniform as a uniform sergeant. Dilemma! I could not become a detective sergeant until I had become an experienced detective constable. So, I put aside my promotion to sergeant for several years until I had enough experience to become a detective sergeant. Promotion in the CID at this time was slow due to the requirement for experience in what was regarded as a specialist role in each rank. (About ten years later, all this changed, and experience no longer became necessary). At about this time, I applied for an accelerated promotion at Bramshill Police College in

Hampshire. Through this route, I would have become a uniform police inspector within three years and leapfrog the next ranks. Unfortunately, my application was rejected.

I passed the selection board for detective constable in late 1984 and was transferred back to Barkingside Police Station while I awaited a place at Hendon on a detective constable training course. So, here I was in the CID but not quite a detective constable. I wouldn't have that title until completing my course, which was due to start in June 1985. I was in something of a limbo regarding my life. Had I made the right career decision? I certainly longed for those days back on the crime squad. Now, I was tied to the CID office and wore a suit and tie. The CID was not expected to seek out criminals as I had done on the crime squad but to react to reported crimes and investigate them. Crime was initially reported to uniform officers during their shift. They would attend, a burglary for example, ascertain all the details, and record them. This would then be allocated to a CID officer to investigate. Only the more serious crime such as burglary, deceptions, rape, and serious assaults would be CID's responsibility to investigate. Shoplifters and other minor matters, such as public disorder, would be investigated by the uniform arresting officer. If the uniform officer arrested someone for a serious offence, he would be handed over to the CID for investigation.

Many of the detectives at Barkingside were approaching retirement and not perhaps as driven and enthusiastic as the officers I had worked with on the crime squad. There was certainly a men's club feel to the CID, and I felt that I had yet to be accepted. My first burglary investigation was very strange. It was reported to the police by a couple in their eighties, who had found many items missing when they moved house. They blamed the removal company for stealing the items. I spoke to the couple at their new home. They were very adamant that various items of furniture and tinned food that had gone missing had, in fact, been stolen. I took a lengthy written statement from them and considered my options. The removal company was well established and had been operating in Barkingside for many years. As I neared the end of the lengthy witness statement, the husband told me in a whispered confidence that the removal van had a secret trapdoor to enable the removers to steal the items. I paused; this changed everything. I made my polite excuses and went to see the removal company manager. The removal van, of course, did not have a trap door.

By the next day, the elderly couple had found all their missing items in different parts of their new home. This was not the most exciting and glamorous start to my CID career! But at least I could close the book on that one. I came to realise that there were one or two detectives who the CID office highly valued – not for their diligent tenacity in bringing criminals to justice, but for having the ability to 'square up' difficult crimes. This would often involve sweet-talking a member of the public who had reported a crime but for which there would be no useful end. It might be a marital matter, a family dispute, or even a difference between neighbours. It could be something that would involve a lengthy investigation with no chance of a conviction. A typical example would be a spouse contacting the police to say that the other spouse had stolen or damaged property during divorce proceedings. The motive would not be clear and the truth even more elusive. The police are often contacted to settle disputes even when there is no evidence of criminality. The police, of course, do not demand fees, whereas solicitors do.

I began to realise that, if all the hopeless crimes reported to the CID were each diligently and remorselessly investigated by detectives, there would be no time left to investigate serious crimes. The CID, perhaps without being consciously aware of it, increased police efficiency. This factor was certainly not appreciated or understood by the senior ranks or the Home Office.

One aspect became a source of frustration both to me and my CID colleagues. Uniform officers expected us to work wonders following their arrests, even when there was no evidence to justify a court appearance. For instance, uniform officers would arrest a man near the scene of a burglary. He may have been evasive in his responses or, in fact, had to be chased as he had run away. He may have had previous court convictions for burglary. In fact, he may well have been the burglar. His arrest would certainly have been justified in these circumstances. To justify to court, however, would require far more evidence. To convince a court that the accused was guilty, the evidence would have to be beyond all reasonable doubt. The reluctance of the CID to take matters further in these circumstances was a cause of some friction with the uniform officers. It was sometimes suggested that the CID were lazy, incompetent, or had taken a bribe. I admit that when I was a uniform officer, I, too, felt that way sometimes.

In some ways, the CID performed the role of the Crown Prosecution Service. We assessed the evidence as being likely or otherwise to achieve a successful prosecution at court.

While waiting for my CID course at Hendon,

which was due to start in June 1985, I gathered further CID experience at Barkingside. This experience related to the investigation of serious crime and CID culture. I was unaware of any corruption by anyone in the CID, nor were there any rumours. It seemed clear to me that corruption was very much a one-off occurrence. My only encounter so far had been with the greyhound owner while I was on the crime squad. He involved no one else. My perception was soon to change.

My CID course at Hendon Detective Training School was very thorough and lasted for four months, but I found it to tedious for most of the time. I had already covered most of the subjects during my five-year service. Some aspects went into far too much detail. I seem to remember that it was technically possible to dishonestly handle stolen property in eighteen different ways. We spent several days on this needless complexity.

Due to a lack of accommodation at Hendon College, we were bussed daily to accommodation at Kingsbury several miles away. I was glad to see the end of the course. I was a pain in the neck to the instructors as I was perhaps too arrogant and smart for my own good. I was at my professional peak – so I thought – and too good to be lectured to.

Detective Constable West Ham CID 1985–88
CID Corruption

I was then posted to West Ham CID in East London. I arrived at West Ham Police station on Monday, the 7th October 1985, as a very shiny, brand-new detective constable. The police station was situated in West ham Lane, near the magistrate's court and Stratford shopping centre. It was a ten-minute walk from Stratford tube station on the Central Line.

This was the day after the Broadwater Farm riots in Tottenham, during which PC Keith Blakelock had been murdered. Oddly as it now seems, I had been unaware of the riots until I reported for duty at West Ham Police Station. This was at a time with no 24-hour rolling news. We were all deeply shocked – not just by his murder but also by the savagery of his murderers. There was anger in the police that police firearms officers had not been deployed, although they were on standby close to the riots. Officers had been fired upon from the walkways of the Broadwater Farm estate prior to PC Blakelock's murder. There had been a reluctance of senior police officers to act decisively. Superintendents and above had dithered when confronted with community race issues. There was a rumour that a named police superintendent in the incident control room monitoring the riot had been punched in the face by a junior officer due to this dithering. There was also a rumour that the police would have thrown rioters off the balconies if the rioting had gone on for a second night. Of course, emotions were high in the police.

What does a detective constable do? His basic role is to investigate serious crimes and bring the offenders to justice. He has the same rank as a uniform police constable and has no supervisory responsibilities within the police. However, as with his uniform colleagues, his responsibilities can be immense when dealing with crime scenes and other such incidents. It is often not appreciated that a police constable takes control and manages serious incidents until assistance arrives. This could be a murder scene, a fatal road collision, or some other serious incident.

By this time of my posting to West Ham, I had

moved with my family from the rather small semi-detached house in Barkingside to a more upmarket 'semi' on the outskirts of Epping in Essex. The reason I made this move was that, in a year or so, my son was to attend the local comprehensive school, and I didn't consider it a favourable option for various reasons. To pay for the more expensive house, I had obtained quite a large mortgage based on my hefty overtime payments on the crime squad at Wanstead. This was the 1980s, and mortgages were easy to obtain. What could ever possibly go wrong? we all thought. Would not house prices keep rising forever.

Even with a Central Line tube station located at Epping, the door-to-door journey to West Ham police station would usually take about ninety minutes. The CID nickname for a tube train was 'the rattler'. Officers from other police forces were often critical of the extra pay that Met officers received and regarded it as unfair. However, most Met officers with children lived outside London, as most state schools there were of such a low standard. The alternative was private education, but the cost was far beyond a police officer's salary.

So, the average commute to work for a Met officer was about ninety minutes. If a tube line wasn't available at either end of their journey to work, the officer would have had to drive. The cost in fuel and wear and tear on his car would have exceeded the extra pay. Also, we must not forget the three-hour return journey daily. This, of course, assumes no delays due to road closures, amount of traffic, and accidents, which would sometimes dramatically increase the journey time or even double it. When driving to work, I frequently had to park my car up to a mile away from the police station due to grid-locked traffic.

My first day as a new detective at West Ham was quite a shock: no one was there apart from me and another detective. He had arrived fresh from Detective Training School about two weeks before me; all the rest of the detectives had been posted away to various murder investigations. This created some concern in my mind. The two of us in the CID office were expected to investigate over thirty serious crimes reported every day. These crimes involved violent muggings (street robbery), rape, burglary, serious assaults, and deceptions. We also dealt with prisoners handed over to us by the uniform officers for interview and investigation. The two of us were also expected to work a shift from 8 am to 10 pm daily. We learned fast. By 10.10 pm, we were in the Bakers Arms – the local pub – for a medicinal pint or three. After a hard day's work, beer never tasted better. The last tube was at about 11.30 pm. We usually ended up having to run to make it on time!

After a few weeks of this onslaught, several detectives returned to the CID office having been released from their murder investigations, and the pressure started to ease.

The Krays were fondly remembered by many West Ham residents. The Krays were two brothers who ran a criminal gang that ruled with fear both the east end and much of London during the 1960s. In some ways, they have become legends. They organised protection rackets and murders. They were imprisoned for life in 1969. I frequently heard residents say that there were no muggings when the Krays were around as they wouldn't put up with it. It was also said that you could leave your front door unlocked, as the Krays would also not tolerate burglary. The violence of the Krays was excused because it was said that they only hurt their own and would never ever hurt a woman or child. If only all this had been true, there would have been no need for the police.

At about this time, I noticed regular muggings taking place near Plaistow tube station. A gang of youths would pounce upon evening commuters as they walked home across the park after dark. Some of the muggers would carry pieces of wood as a weapon. I devised a plan to deal with them. I requested help from the uniform sergeant who managed the beat crime team. He was helpful and offered several of his team to assist. He also found three home beat uniform officers to help. I would describe this sergeant as a good sort; he was very sensible and had a great sense of humour. My plan was to find an observation point and watch as commuters walked across the park, which was dimly lit at night. I found a walkway on one of the adjacent block of flats that gave me a clear view. I deployed the officers around the park in plain clothes, and we were all in radio contact with each other. After only about ten minutes, I saw a man in a suit walking across the park from the rail station carrying a briefcase. All at once, six youths appeared out of the shadows, jumped on him, and stole his briefcase. I gave the command to arrest, and the nearby officers swooped and arrested them all; three of the muggers were armed with small wooden staves. The briefcase was found, and there were no more muggings there after this. It was a good example of teamwork and showed what could be achieved with only a few officers.

The trial of these muggers began at Snaresbrook Crown Court several months later. All the muggers denied the offence, stating it was a case of mistaken identity by the arresting officers! I was, therefore, cross-examined in the witness box by six defence barristers in turn. This was quite gruelling. All suggested that I had also been mistaken. The court would not allow me to mention that three of the muggers had been carrying sticks as weapons, as this might have prejudiced the jury. Anyway, five were found guilty by the jury, and the sixth was found not guilty. The jury was visibly angry when they learned that the youth who they had found not guilty had, in fact, been carrying a weapon.

By now, I had noticed that, no matter how successful at court I was, no one else cared. I could spend a week or more at the Crown Court working hard and giving evidence only to find that the police had no interest in the result. One reason for this was that the police were not assessed upon the results at court. If an accused was either found guilty or acquitted, it did not make any difference to police performance statistics. Another reason was that, by the time a case came to trial at the Crown Court, it could be six months or more old. A week is a long time in the CID, and life moves on very quickly.

It is worth briefly explaining what happens to you if you are unfortunate enough to be arrested. A police officer only needs a small amount of evidence to arrest you but much more evidence to send you to court. Some officers find it difficult to make arrests and are often held back by indecision and a lack of self-confidence. After all, by making an arrest, a police officer is depriving someone of their liberty; this is a serious matter. I never suffered these doubts.

When a police officer arrests you, he should explain why you are being arrested and caution you that you do not have to say anything from this time onwards. You are then taken to a police station. There, the sergeant in the custody suite will enter all your details in the station record and check that your arrest is justified by briefly questioning the arresting officer in your presence. You will then be searched to make sure you do not have anything on you that could harm you or others. (The arresting officer may already have done this when you were arrested). You will then be asked if you require a solicitor. If you are unemployed, you will not have to pay for a solicitor to attend the police station, give you advice, and sit with you during a police interview. However, if you are employed, you will probably have to pay, and this can be quite costly.

At this point, the police would investigate the offence for which you were arrested. You will almost certainly be interviewed by the police about the offence. This interview will be recorded; it is your right not to answer any questions. After their investigation is completed, which usually takes a few hours, the decision will be made whether to release you or charge you and send you to court. Release without any further action by the police happens to about half the people who are arrested. If you are released, this doesn't necessarily mean the police have made a mistake in arresting you, although that can occasionally be the case. For instance, a witness to the crime may refuse to give a written statement to the police and would not, therefore, attend court to give evidence against you. As I mentioned earlier, only a small amount of evidence is required to justify in law an arrest.

To take things further and send someone to court takes a lot more evidence. If the evidence is available, you may be charged. To be charged means that the custody suite sergeant will read the offence, which you are alleged to have committed, out to you and send this with your details to the court for a hearing in front of the magistrate. The charge must be authorised by the Crown Prosecution Service to ensure there is sufficient evidence to have at least a 51% chance of a successful prosecution at court. You may then be released from the police station but must appear at the magistrates on a date set soon into the future. However, if the charge relates to murder or something serious, you may have to stay at the police station overnight and face the magistrates in the morning. The custody sergeant would not want to release you in case you left the country to evade justice or perhaps go on to commit another serious crime.

There are time limits regarding how long an arrested person can be detained at a police station. These time limits can be extended if the Crown Prosecution Service makes an application in court to a magistrate. These time limits can be extended further if you are arrested for terrorism. The reasons for these extensions are mainly to conduct identity parades and to await forensic evidence from the science laboratories.

Assuming that the custody sergeant has charged you with a crime, you will now enter the judicial system. The judicial system can seem confusing at first, but it is generally quite simple. The court that deals with about 80% of criminal offences is the magistrates court. All criminal cases, including murder, start here. Most of the larger towns have a magistrates court. There is no judge or jury; two or three magistrates sit together and decide upon the guilt or otherwise of the accused person. The longest period in prison that magistrates can impose is one year. Magistrates have no legal qualifications but do have to attend courses of instruction. For instance, if you are charged with murder, you will appear first at the magistrates court, and your case will be sent to the Crown Court to be dealt with by a judge and jury. The sentence for murder is, of course, far more than the maximum of a year that the magistrates could sentence you to.

The Crown Court has a judge and jury. The jury decides whether or not you are guilty. The judge advises the jury on points of law and decides upon your sentence if the jury finds you guilty.

The Old Bailey is also a Crown Court. Some of the judges at the Old Bailey can sentence you to a greater imprisonment term than at the other Crown Courts. The Old Bailey also acts as an overflow if Crown Courts in the area are full.

The above is very much a simplification of the judicial system, and it is far more complex than my summary. However, if you have understood the above, you are doing well!

It was not unusual for a West Ham detective to attend the local hospital to ask to see the victim of a stabbing and to be asked by a nurse to specify which one as there were several being treated. Most stabbing victims refused to contact the police and preferred to be treated anonymously in hospital casualty. Most stabbings were not in police records for this very reason. I remember walking through Stratford shopping mall one morning on my way to work and seeing a large pool of blood and bandages. I fully expected a murder enquiry to take place, but nothing had been reported to the police.

An unusual offence took place in 1986. A young woman standing at a bus stop in Stratford one morning had a length of her hair cut off by a man with a pair of scissors as he walked past. She was a fashion model and was obviously upset at this. He then indecently assaulted her and ran off. This is not a unique offence, and a number are reported to the police every year. Hairdressers often experience men sneaking into the shop and grabbing clumps of hair off the floor before running away. She provided an e-fit of the man, and it matched the face of a man known to us. He was a petty criminal. She identified him on an identity parade. He denied the offence but was charged and later appeared in court. The jury did not find him guilty, and he was acquitted. To this day, I am not sure if it was him, but the evidence gave us no option but to charge him.

Also in 1986, I investigated the arrest of three youths who had been involved in 'muggings'. From their description, I suspected them of having committed many such crimes in the Stratford area of West Ham. One youth was aged sixteen, and I interviewed him in the presence of his father. I suggested he and the other two had committed many muggings. I showed him a list of muggings that probably related to him. He decided to admit to about thirty such offences. At this point, my colleague stopped the interview and told the father that he should get a solicitor, as these were serious matters. My colleague had many years of CID experience. The father agreed, and the youth was released. We interviewed him about a week later. With him were his father and now a solicitor. To every question I put to the youth, he now replied 'no comment'. This was very frustrating, but there was nothing that could be done about it. Technically, there was no need for a solicitor as the youth had his father with him. He was only charged with one mugging and received at court what is commonly known as a 'slap on the wrist'.

In April 1986, an event occurred that was to change my life. I was confronted with blatant criminal corruption committed by my supervisor, a detective sergeant. He had been transferred from a neighbouring police station by our detective chief inspector (DCI). The DCI was not satisfied with his work output, so he paired this detective sergeant with me, as he thought I would be able to manage him and monitor his performance. I felt complimented to be entrusted with this task. I think the DCI intuitively realised that all was not well with this detective sergeant. The DCI was a very astute judge of people and situations. He was one of the best leaders I have ever worked with. This DCI was Bill Griffiths who retired as a deputy assistant commissioner – one rank higher than that of deputy chief constable. It's a shame he was not selected to be commissioner of the Met.

About a fortnight later, I was working with the detective sergeant on a late shift. This shift ran from 2 pm to 10 pm. At about 6 pm, two uniform officers arrested a suspected drug dealer in his car and brought him to West Ham Police Station. The dealer had £1,000 in banknotes in a briefcase. Additionally, he had a flick knife and a small quantity of cocaine, probably for 'sample' purposes. Also in the car were a few stolen credit cards. The dealer was driving his own new Mercedes Sports coupe. This was a good arrest. I spoke to the arresting officers and complimented them. This dealer was now to be investigated by the detective sergeant and me. The dealer had a couple of previous criminal convictions for minor offences but nothing significant. However, he was suspected by various agencies as being a major dealer in drugs. Quite often, the top criminal echelons do not have numerous criminal convictions; the police tend to be good at catching the minor players.

The dealer did not want a solicitor. The detective sergeant interviewed the dealer, and I recorded the interview in ink on blank forms provided for this purpose. At the end, he would be invited to sign each page if he agreed with its content. (Tape recorders had not yet been introduced for interviews). The interview had barely commenced when the detective sergeant recognised the dealer from a previous arrest when he was in Plaistow CID several years before. The dealer had been involved in the theft of a lorry load of goods. The detective sergeant had corruptly dealt with him and secured his release without charge in return for a cash payment.

A friendly conversation took place between the two. I was surprised at all this. During the conversation, the detective sergeant asked the dealer if it would be the same 'arrangement' as on the last occasion they had met in Plaistow. The dealer agreed, and the detective sergeant said it would all depend on my attitude to this. The detective sergeant invited me to leave the interview with him to explain the plan he had in mind. He explained that he and I could split the dealer's £1,000 between us in return for 'losing' the evidence against the dealer and releasing him that evening. The dealer was happy to part with the £1,000 for this purpose. The proposal was that the dealer would hand over the money to us once he had been released from the police station. The detective sergeant then said he needed to talk to the dealer about it all a little more. I said I had to phone my wife and would be back in about ten minutes. On my own now, I thought about all the implications. I had not expected this. I only had a minute or two to decide what to do. I realised that if I reported this, my life would change forever and not necessarily for the better. However, I did not want to be 'bought' by a career criminal. It went against every principle of being a police officer. Honesty and integrity are paramount. I also thought that if I reported it, it would set a precedent and make it easier for detectives to do the same in the future. As far as I was aware then, no detective had ever taken such action against a corrupt superior officer.

I decided to immediately report the situation to the Met's Complaint Section. There was no going back now.

I was fitted with a covert recording device and returned to the interview about an hour later. My excuse to the detective sergeant regarding my absence was that I had a family matter to deal with, and he accepted that. The interview with the dealer started again, and this time, the detective sergeant not only asked the questions but also provided the answers for me to write down. The detective sergeant designed these fabricated answers to lessen the severity of the crime. I was now performing an undercover role. Although I had had no undercover training, I knew that I should not ask leading questions that could force the detective sergeant to incriminate himself. However, sufficient evidence was needed. The conviction of police officers for corruption was rare and difficult to achieve. I acted slightly confused and asked the detective sergeant to explain what was going to happen next. He said that the plan was all ready to go: we would get the money in the police station car park when the dealer was released and went to pick up his impounded car. I made my excuses and reported this update to the complaints team. I then had to write a long statement about all these events. This was in case the recording device had malfunctioned. I had a small scotch provided by the chief superintendent in his office before I drove home. We joked that it would be ironic if I was breathalysed. The detective sergeant was suspended from duty later that evening.

Overnight, someone had placed a very offensive handwritten note on my desk regarding my actions. A colleague told me about the note and destroyed it before I could read it. About a month later, I noticed a small clear plastic bag of cannabis in one of my desk drawers that already had a broken lock. Was it there to incriminate me? I held it up for all to see in the office, then I threw it in the bin. Should I have reported it? I'd had enough of police corruption by then.

About a year later, the detective sergeant stood trial at the Old Bailey for corruption. A detective constable was nominated to accompany me as protection: it was feared that someone might want to throw me in front of a tube train or bus on the way to the Old Bailey.

Standing in the dock with the detective sergeant was the dealer. Both stated that they were not guilty, and I was therefore required to give evidence to the court from the witness stand. I felt as though I also was on trial. I was not allowed to speak to the prosecution barrister, and I only had a few minutes to read my complex statement to refresh my memory. My attempt at giving my evidence did not go well as I confused some of my evidence. This was probably due to the pressure and lack of an opportunity to study my statement. The trial was stopped and started again about two months later. During this interval, I went to the Met Police video and sound laboratory and checked the recording again. The recording was muffled at times, but on this occasion, I was able to clearly hear more incriminating evidence. These additional pieces of evidence were provided to both the CPS and the defence solicitors. When the case was next at the Old Bailey, the detective sergeant decided to plead guilty rather than fight the case. This was probably due to the additional evidence the laboratory identified.

He was sentenced to six months imprisonment. By the standards of today, that was a very lenient sentence. The case against the dealer was dropped: he was the only real winner out of the three of us.

The West Ham local newspaper's front-page headline stated that a CID 'grass' had caused the conviction. This was not the best choice of wording, in my view. About twelve years later, I received an assistant commissioner's commendation for 'integrity, leadership, courage, and commitment in a confidential enquiry'.

West Ham CID was now short of a detective sergeant. As I had passed the promotion examination, I was nominated to be an acting detective sergeant. There was no extra pay. I held this rank until I was officially promoted two years later as a uniform sergeant.

Anyway, the tsunami of crime continued at West Ham. There was no pause or truce. This was probably a good thing as it kept my mind occupied with little time to dwell on my actions. Although I had done the right thing, I felt guilty: I had sent a fellow police officer to prison. Nobody among my fellow officers said that I had done the wrong thing, but I was now aware that I had become someone different in their eyes. Or was I becoming paranoid? Being among those I had worked with was helpful to me; they knew the facts about what had happened. There were opportunities to transfer elsewhere for a fresh start. Beyond West Ham, some bizarre rumours circulated about the incident. One was that I had reported the corrupt detective sergeant for not providing me with a big enough share of the money. Another rumour was that I had agreed to the corrupt deal but had lost my nerve further down the line and reported his actions to protect myself. Many CPS lawyers assumed that all the CID was completely corrupt anyway and that I must have had a personal vendetta against the detective sergeant to have taken the action I did. There were also a few comments from long-serving detectives that the detective sergeant brought it upon himself for naively expecting a new detective constable to readily agree with his plan. This only served to muddy the already cloudy waters of morality.

Did I regret my actions? In some ways, yes, I did. But I had been put in a terrible situation. I had great loyalty to my fellow officers, but his corruption crossed the line. If I had simply said to the detective sergeant, "Go ahead, but don't include me", I would still have been as guilty as him of corruption. Also, he could have possibly acted the same way the following week. Having ignored him the first time, how would I deal with his second and no doubt third act of corruption to follow? I would have had to go along with it. In my view, corruption becomes a cancer that, if unchecked, devours police officers and undermines the police service.

A few weeks later, I was walking up the stairs from the custody suite to the CID office. I had to pass the interview room at the top of the stairs. This room was used to interview people about the offence for which they had been arrested. As I walked past, I heard a woman shouting about how her son must not be interviewed. She sounded aggressive. I opened the door to check what was happening. It was not my business to do this – I was not a supervisor – but I felt that it was my duty to do so. I saw two uniform officers speaking to a youth with a woman present. I asked the officers if everything was okay; they said it was. I politely asked the woman to stop shouting. I then shut the door and left all four of them in the room. I thought nothing more about it. About two weeks later, a message was sent to all officers asking who the plain-clothed officer was who had intervened during an interview. I volunteered my details. I did not have to do this, but I had done nothing wrong, and I did not anticipate a problem. How mistaken I was.

The mother of the youth being interviewed was a member of the Newham Police Monitoring Group. She stated in her complaint that I had dragged her out of the interview room, swung her around my body, and thrown her down the stairs to the custody suite.

I was interviewed about this by a chief inspector from the complaints unit and his colleague. He told me that everything would be okay if I admitted it. I denied that anything had happened. I told him about my experience with the corrupt detective sergeant, and he said, "Oh, it was you!" in a disdainful manner.

I ended up undergoing what was known as an 'informal resolution' with this woman while under the supervision of the complaints unit. This process was supposed to allow both parties to resolve their differences via a meaningful discussion. Also present during this discussion were the two uniform officers who had been involved in the interview I had interrupted. Both officers had supported my account of events. I asked her if there was a political motivation for making this unfounded allegation. There was not enough room to swing a cat in the area she alleged I had spun her around in. I asked her for evidence of injuries that would have incurred if she had been flung down the stairs. I asked what her son had to say about this. There was no response from her. The complaints unit terminated the process. Whether this counted against me or not, I had no idea.

What really annoyed me was that, if I had assaulted her, I would never have responded to the request from the complaints unit; they had no idea who it was. Looking back, I should not have bothered for all the unnecessary aggravation it caused me. What was also annoying was the assumption by the complaints' unit chief inspector that I was guilty of assault.

West Ham Police Station's area included Stratford. This area had no resemblance to Stratford upon Avon, the home of Shakespeare. No resemblance at all. Eastend Stratford was known as 'Stabbing City'. Stabbings were often used as an Eastend warning for breaking the code of acceptable behaviour. Whatever the code was, it was never made clear. Often, the stabbings would be inflicted on the top of the leg or buttocks. Although intended to cause pain and discomfort, it was not always done with the intention to murder. However, those who inflicted these injuries were not known to have the precision of NHS surgeons. As a result, a few bled to death. This death would result in a murder investigation. Those who did not die rarely expected the police to investigate, as they would 'sort it out' themselves in due course. Unsurprisingly, the following week, the assailant would be stabbed as retribution and end up in hospital. He, too, would not request police action. This tit for tat could go on for some time.

Had it not been for paramedics, the murder rate at West Ham and nationally would have been a lot higher. Paramedics would attend and stabilise a stabbing victim's condition. This prevented him from dying from blood loss before arrival at the hospital.

The following typified this Eastend culture. On Christmas Day 1986, I was on duty as an acting detective sergeant. There was just me and a detective constable on duty. Just after the queen's speech had ended, a uniform inspector came into the CID office and announced that there had been a stabbing at a local public house. This was now my responsibility to investigate. I was a hardened, grim-faced detective by now, with just over a year's experience. I drove to the pub: it was a scene of carnage. All the windows had been smashed, and there were abandoned knives on the windowsills. An ambulance crew was wheeling out a man who had a deep, wide cut to his throat. He told me he had tripped and fallen on his way to the bar and accidentally sliced open his throat on some broken glass on the floor. He was obviously signed up to the East London code of silence. By the standards of the day, no actual crime had been committed, as the victim refused to substantiate it and provide a written statement. I left and went back to my paperwork.

Today, the system would require seizing his clothes as potential court exhibits, taking a witness statement – no matter how pointless – from him, cordoning off the pub, requesting photographers, exhibits officers, and forensic scientists, taking lengthy witness statements from those in the pub, and compiling a very lengthy report. My point is that nothing would have been gained by expensively and extensively investigating this crime. I had saved the public a vast amount of money and time.

One evening after a long day, I was about to interview a suspect for a serious assault when I noticed through the window a group of men gathered around the driver's door of a police van at the front of the police station. One opened the driver's door and stole a police helmet from the dashboard. They all then ran off. I dashed down the stairs to the custody suite to inform the officers there. They gave chase. The helmet was recovered, and all of them were given a blunt verbal warning by the officers as to their actions. The officer should have locked the van. I had saved him some embarrassment, and he would possibly have had to pay for the cost of a replacement helmet.

In 1987, I dealt with a disturbing case of paedophilia. I was in the CID office when another detective took a phone call from a member of the social services. A report had been made to them about a man at a local address suspected of sexually abusing young girls. I decided that immediate action was called for. I saw no value in investigating this further or seeking a search warrant, as this would be time wasted while children were at risk of further serious sexual assaults. I took two other officers to the address. I was prepared to force open the door if it wasn't immediately answered. An elderly man answered the door. Children had been present, as evidenced by toys and clothes scattered around. I arrested him on suspicion of sexually assaulting young girls under ten. He was taken to West Ham Police Station for detention and interview.

As a father, I found my investigation to be particularly offensive. The man I had arrested was eighty-seven years old and 'friend' to a vulnerable single mother of daughters under the age of ten. In the past, he had sexually abused the mother when she was a child. He was not the father of these children. My investigation revealed years of horrific sexual abuse of these children. Often the mother was present during the assaults to provide 'reassurance' to her frightened kids. I cannot detail the nature of these offences as it offends me even now after all these years.

There was a particular piece of evidence I found to help secure his conviction at the Old Bailey. This item was a large, handwritten diary he had kept during his sexual assaults. Unfortunately, his handwritten entries relating to his assaults on these girls were in code. The code was a complex mixture of Greek and Russian alphabet. He was a highly educated man and an author of a book that encouraged paedophilia. I needed to crack this code: it stood in the way of convicting a serial paedophile.

A detective sergeant in the CID office had an idea: he had been on the Anti-Terrorist Branch at New Scotland Yard for several years, and so he submitted a copy of the diary to Special Branch. They forwarded it to MI5. (MI5 didn't officially exist then). A few days later, I received information that would enable me to decode the diary. The comments from MI5 were that the author was highly intelligent as it was a complex code to crack. I spent my lunchtime breaks decoding the diary – it was the only time I was free from CID office distraction. It revealed detailed sexual abuse of these children and was personally written by him in ink. It was a form of written evidential confession.

To date, he had denied all the offences put to him in his interview, and he only spoke in general terms about paedophilia. There was a serious problem, however, that would stop me from using this damning evidence in court. Due to their secretive existence, MI5 could not give me a signed written statement that would prove their decoding of the diaries. This was vital for court. They also could not attend court. The only solution was to ask the paedophile about this in an interview and see if he would confirm the MI5 decoding. This was going to be tricky.

This paedophile was a very vain and arrogant man. He had previously stated in general terms that there was nothing wrong with sexually abusing children if they consented. The children he sexually abused clearly stated that they had certainly not consented. I had to remain objective, polite, and detached when dealing with him, no matter how I felt inside. I was still subconsciously following the advice of my sergeant from when I was a recruit at Hendon.

When I next interviewed him, I appealed to

his intellectual vanity. I said that his code in the diary was superb and took a long time to crack. I quoted a few examples of the code, and he agreed that I was right. This was now enough to allow his 'confessions' in the diary to be used as evidence. Also, there was no need to expose the existence of MI5.

A few months later, this paedophile appeared at the Old Bailey for trial. He pleaded not guilty to all the offences with which he was indicted. This meant the children would have to appear in court in front of him and give evidence in public. This was a tactical move by his defence team to put pressure on the children. A deal was struck by the court. He admitted to being guilty of far less serious offences. In return, the children were spared from the trauma of giving evidence. The paedophile only received a sentence of four years imprisonment. He would have been out after only two years or less for good behaviour. This was not a satisfactory conclusion, and I felt that justice had not been done.

Today, the Met has a dedicated team investigating sexual abuse against children. They are swamped with work; digital technology has exposed so much crime of this nature.

A law-abiding and honest resident of West Ham decided to advertise his car for sale in the local newspaper. What could possibly go wrong?

Three men answered his classified advertisement and asked for a test drive. The owner went with them in the car as security. After less than a couple of minutes of driving, they attacked the owner and threw him out of his car before driving off. The owner picked himself up and staggered back to his home. When he got there, he discovered that his front door had been forced open and the house ransacked. He never got his car back.

What makes a leader, and what makes a manager? Much has been written over the years to define both. My simple definition is that a leader is so inspirational that their people will willingly follow them into danger. A manager will convene a meeting to discuss the overall implications and refer the conclusions to another manager. Meanwhile, the danger will have passed, and the manager and their fellow managers will congratulate themselves on having provided 'public reassurance' to the community with a successful police operation. I have worked with a few magnificent leaders in the police. Of these few, only two made it to high rank. The police prefer to promote those who can be relied upon to support Met policy, even if they don't agree with it. In other words, 'yes people'. Another term used is 'cabinet responsibility'. Practical experience and ability count for nothing. Very few officers of senior rank have been to Crown Court to give evidence and would be terrified if called upon to do so.

One morning as I arrived for work at West Ham, I noticed that my way into the station yard at the rear of the building was obstructed by police tape clearly stating 'do not cross'. I assumed this was some sort of error or joke, and I walked under it. I reached the back door and went upstairs to the CID office. I sat at my desk, and someone asked if I had seen it. I gave a blank look. I was then told that a petrol bomb had been thrown into the rear yard and destroyed several cars. I looked out of the window, and there were the burnt-out vehicles clear to see. Oh well, I thought, that's West Ham for you.

A detective sergeant I worked with at West Ham made quite a name for himself during the following incident. He was engaged on one of West Ham's many murder investigations during which the team had met a wall of silence, with no witnesses willing to come forward and help the police. He went into a particular pub with a detective constable to give them a piece of his mind. At the bar, he turned to the assembled drinkers and, in a loud and authoritative voice, declared that he would close the pub within a week if no witnesses came forward. He told them that their behaviour was disgraceful and that they ought all to be ashamed of themselves.

He paused for effect before striding to what he thought was the exit door, opened it, and found himself in a broom cupboard. The detective constable did not have a code of silence and happened to mention it to all on the team.

In 1987, a jeweller was murdered in his shop in Stratford Broadway, E15. One early morning, the jeweller raised the shutters outside his small shop and entered the premises. Two men, one armed with a hidden sawn-off shotgun, followed him inside. The jeweller was alone. He was made to kneel before then being shot in the head and dying. Jewellery was then stolen, and the two men made off on foot.

This was the execution of an innocent man in cold blood. I joined the murder team based in an office at West Ham. The team was supervised by an experienced detective superintendent from elsewhere and composed of about twelve detectives. A small number of uniform officers were working in plainclothes, mainly from the local crime squad. We set to work with determination to catch the killers. In those days, there was no CCTV, and we had to rely on forensic clues and underworld informants. I think there was a feeling among the local criminals that this murder was beyond the pale. Not only that, but the police would now start lifting stones and shining their torches in gloomy areas of the criminal underworld. Life was now going to become hot for the criminal fraternity unless the murderers were found.

Within a day or so, an established criminal informant contacted West Ham police and provided the names of the murderers. Of course, he was not prepared to attend court and give evidence. This information was exactly what we had been waiting for. Search warrants were immediately obtained from a magistrate. Both these murderers had a history of criminality and violence. Armed officers raided both of their addresses at dawn; this prevented one of the murderers from contacting the other to make good an escape. Both men were taken by surprise and escorted to West Ham Police Station. No gun had been found – neither had any stolen jewellery. We had found the right men, but we needed evidence to charge them.

I, along with a colleague, interviewed one of the men. My colleague recorded the questions and answers in ink as I spoke. (There were no tape recordings as standard at that time). My assessment of him was that he was not the killer. He was facing a murder charge, nevertheless. My approach was successful, and he admitted that he was present at the murder but that his accomplice had fired the shotgun and murdered the jeweller. He had not expected this to happen, and it was not part of their plan. He also told me where the jewellery they had not sold was dumped – in a builder's skip in Bow several miles away. We later found the items of jewellery in the skip, all with tags identifying them as being from the jeweller's shop. He also admitted his part in a bank robbery some weeks earlier, where a gun had been used. Without his confession to me that included where the jewellery had been discarded, the case would never have been solved.

At that time, the police could refuse access to a solicitor if it was feared that they would intentionally or otherwise alert other suspects regarding the serious offence. In this case, he was refused access to a solicitor, and no solicitor was present during the interview. Today, due to a change in the law, a solicitor cannot be refused access. If a solicitor had been present during the interview, advising him to say nothing, would he have fully admitted the offence? I don't think he would have. The change in the law has made the job of the investigating detective that much harder.

His accomplice was being interviewed elsewhere at the same time and admitted his involvement but to a far lesser degree. Both were charged with murder and firearm offences. Too dangerous to be released on bail, they were remanded in custody awaiting trial at the Old Bailey.

While in prison awaiting trial, both appeared at West Ham magistrates court regarding a bail application. During this hearing, the one who had fired the gun took a member of court staff hostage. He used a toothbrush with a razor attached as a weapon. These were different times compared to today. I and my colleagues rushed him while he was distracted and pinned him to the ground. He probably suffered a few bruises. The hostage was released unharmed. I don't think we took any action regarding this incident. He was facing serious charges, and this incident would not have seen the light of day at court.

Some months later, both murderers stood trial at the Old Bailey. The defence case seemed to concentrate on alleged police procedural flaws. However, both were found guilty by the jury. The father of the murdered jeweller approached me outside the courtroom after the trial and shook my hand, thanking me for my efforts. This was worth more to me than any police commendation.

My service at West Ham CID taught me that our role was complex. I spent my time 'spinning plates', trying to balance so many demands at once. For a uniform officer, everything was handed over to the next shift. I could not do that as a CID officer. Everything stayed with me. Every day, I gained more 'spinning-plates'. The art was never to drop a plate; the science was to recognise the priorities. So many crimes were reported to us that we had to find a way to prioritise what was evidentially viable and what was not.

Help was at hand. On 1st April 1986, the Crown Prosecution Service (CPS) came into being. Many CID officers were almost offended at the creation of the CPS, as they saw it as taking away their authority. In essence, the CPS was a locally based team of lawyers and staff, who were there to assess the viability or otherwise of police charges. Prior to this, the CID had assumed this role in many ways. I did not see the CPS as a threat; I was used to attending the magistrate's court almost daily with ongoing, complex cases. Now, the CPS would do this for me, and I could concentrate on my many other investigations.

On this day in April 1986, when the CPS was created, I happened to be in the magistrates court at West Ham. I was waiting to object to the release of a criminal who was on remand in prison awaiting trial at the Crown Court. When the case was called, I stepped forward from my seat at the back to head for the witness box, my bail objections in hand. I was primed and ready for a verbal fight with the defence solicitor. A petite woman dressed in black blocked my path. She said she was a lawyer from the CPS and she would be dealing with this. I was shocked. There was a moment or two before I very reluctantly allowed her to usurp my role. In many ways, this symbolised how the CPS had become the new prosecuting authority overnight.

We in the CID hoped that the CPS would be similar in role to the American District Attorney's office. The role of the American District Attorney's office was to work with the police in their investigations and provide advice. It transpired that the role of the CPS was not to actively assist the police in their investigations but to assess the viability of evidence.

However, I decided to seek the advice of the CPS at an early stage in one of my investigations. The CPS had been in existence for perhaps a week or so. It was a complex case. In essence, there had been a fight at a petrol station between the occupants of two cars who were disputing access to a specific petrol pump. It was a minor matter, but it resulted in multiple GBH assaults with no clear evidence as to which party was to blame. Both parties used hand weapons. There was no CCTV available; to fully investigate this would have taken weeks of police time. My view was that the occupants of both cars were as bad as each other and that the CPS would have dropped the case anyway, even when fully investigated. The case was reviewed by a CPS lawyer with the Stratford CPS, and she agreed with my assessment. The investigation was therefore terminated. My workload was high, and I didn't want to waste my time investigating a case that was doomed to failure. In this respect, I found the CPS to be of significant value. I rarely found them to be a cause of personal frustration. The officers most vocal in their condemnation of the CPS tended to be those who either did not understand the law or had not fully prepared their case file before submission to the CPS.

The CID provided a detective constable every night to advise the West Ham uniform shift. Every ten weeks or so, I worked a week of night duty between a Monday and Sunday. I would have a driver from the trainee CID crime squad to assist me. I did rather mainly enjoy these periods of night duty: it was a pleasure to be released from routine investigations and be almost as independent as I was back in 1984 on the Wanstead crime squad in our yellow Austin Metro. One such night duty in the summer of 1987 I will always remember.

The weather was certainly warm that week. The uniform night shift was very competent; we were not required for advice, and no serious incidents occurred. This left me free with my colleague to patrol and seek out the criminals. At about 11 pm one night, we were driving along Romford Road in a plain CID car when I noticed a group of youths on a side road bending wipers on parked cars. We drove on, and I called for help on the radio. Both ends of the side road were sealed off by coordinated uniform vehicles. The group of about six youths was arrested for the trail of damage they had caused. The damage included wing mirrors and wind screen wipers. All were convicted at court.

The next night at about midnight, we were driving in a residential street when we both smelt burning. Was it the car brakes? As we rounded a corner, I saw a crowd of people in the street. A middle terrace house was on fire, flames bursting through the roof. As I stepped from the car, I made an urgent call for the fire service. I was told by the crowd that there was a family inside. I rang the doorbell of the house next door to warn them. There was no reply, so I picked up a dust bin and threw it through the downstairs window. The door was answered, and I warned them to get out. I ran through their house to the back garden. I suspected that the family of the blazing house next door were probably asleep upstairs. I climbed onto the kitchen extension at the rear of the blazing house using a step ladder from nearby. This gave me access to the bedroom window at the rear. I felt the window glass, and it was cold: the fire was in the roof above me. Embers were falling around me. My driver passed the step ladder up to me. He also rather thoughtfully passed me the small green fire extinguisher from our CID car. It was, of course, no use to me. I needed the ladder to break the window and search the room for the occupants who may have been overcome by smoke.

I broke the window using the step ladder's length to protect me from the falling glass. Thick smoke poured out. I quickly cleared as much glass as I could from the window ledge. It was quite high, and I had to grip it with both hands to pull myself over and into the bedroom. I cut my hands on the glass but did not notice the pain at the time. Now inside, I searched the room. I could only breathe by quickly returning to the window and getting some fresh air. There was no one that I could find. By now, I was exhausted and almost fell out of the window onto the kitchen roof. The fire service had arrived, and I could do no more. A fire fighter was below me on the ground, and he reached out his hand to me. I thought he wanted me to help him up, but in fact, he was helping me down. Adrenalin has strange effects.

I was treated in hospital for smoke inhalation and cuts. Nothing could be done for smoke inhalation, but I was checked over anyway. The cuts to my hands were bandaged. It transpired that no one was in the house as they were all out at a family meal. Two uniform officers attended the scene and rescued a caged parrot from the ground floor, which was not affected by fire or smoke. The local newspaper ran with the headline that uniform officers had rescued a parrot from a burning house. I was not mentioned. The uniform sergeant on duty that night shift recommended me for a commendation, but nothing transpired. No matter, I did my best. We all did.

On the Friday night at about 11 pm, we parked across the road from 'The Two Puddings' night club in Stratford Broadway, West Ham. Shortly afterwards, a large man emerged from the club with a woman. An argument started between them, and he began to slap her hard in the face repeatedly. At this point, I decided to intervene. As we stepped from the car, I called West Ham for help on my hand-held police radio. I did not wait for a reply and crossed the busy road. As we reached the couple, I could see that it would not be an easy matter to restrain him. I told him to stop hitting this woman, and I took hold of one of his arms. His arm was wider than my leg. He threw me to one side, and I ended up face down on the pavement. The same happened to my colleague. I called on the radio again for help. West Ham Police Station was about six hundred yards away and around the next corner. There was still no sign of help. We tried to restrain him again, but the same thing happened. Now, the woman who had been assaulted turned on my colleague by jumping on his back. Many men were now leaving the club and also turned on us with punches and kicks. Things were looking bleak.

At this point, a uniform police officer without his helmet ran around the corner and plunged into the fray. This changed the situation completely. Moments later, a police van appeared with numerous officers to take control of the situation. My relief and joy were short-lived. I had backed up to the railings next to the road for protection. Suddenly, I was grabbed around my neck from behind by a uniform police officer. He very soon recognised me, and I was released with apologies.

It turned out that my radio was faulty, and they only received fragments of my messages for help. It was only upon my fourth attempt that they realised where I was. My thanks are eternal for the officer who appeared at full speed from around the corner and took them all on. I and my colleague suffered quite a few bruises. My colleague had a massive lump of a bruise on his head.

The large man was arrested and turned out to have been an East London heavy-weight boxer in the past, with previous criminal convictions. He was placed in a detention cell but managed to displace the door frame trying to escape. He pleaded not guilty at West Ham magistrates court to charges of assault on me and my colleague. The defence proposed by his lawyer was that he thought my radio was a gun. Thanks to the CPS adjourning the trial for a few minutes, I was able to collect a radio from West Ham Police Station and illustrate to the court that a police radio bore no resemblance to a gun. The magistrates found him guilty, and he received a fine.

This incident never made the local news, but it showed how supportive officers were of each other. It can be a very lonely place on the street when things are going rather badly.

Another night duty incident this time involved murder. At about 1 am, I was notified of the death of a woman in a Stratford shopping mall. The force medical examiner (doctor) and the duty uniform inspector assessed her death as being from a heart attack. I decided that her death was possibly murder. She was what was known as a 'bag lady' – essentially a vagrant.

There were a few blood drops in the vicinity of her body that supposedly related to the heart attack. I discovered that she had been seen with a man just before her death and established his description. I requested the assistance of a dog van and more police units from beyond West Ham to help find him.

He was found on the railway platform at Stratford waiting for a train. He was arrested and taken to West Ham for interview in the morning. A post-mortem the next day established that the 'bag lady' had been kicked to death. The suspect for this murder admitted his involvement to the officers who interviewed him. After having had sex with the 'bag lady' for money, he refused to pay her and killed her. He was found guilty at the Old Bailey and imprisoned. Were it not for my assessment and actions, the murderer would never have been brought to justice.

One night duty, I was called to a pub in nearby Canning Town, where a shooting had recently occurred. I walked into the bar where men were still drinking. A large chunk of wood had been blasted from the bar by a gun. The pub door had also been blown away. Both were undoubtedly caused by a shotgun. I asked the gathered drinkers if they had seen anything suspicious. I did not expect a reply and did not receive one. I asked to see the landlord. He appeared from upstairs. I pointed out the damage, and he looked totally amazed. He turned to me and said, "That's a bit naughty, isn't it?"

On the evening of the 30th August 1987, a murder took place at the Telegraph pub, Church Street, West Ham. A man who had been drinking at the pub was attacked outside in the street. He was stabbed, shot, and had ammonia squirted in his face. The top of his skull was also removed with a blow from an axe. He died in the street. It appeared that the incident started in the pub, as a spent bullet was found embedded in the floor. We were provided with the name of a suspect for the murder. I and two colleagues went to a terraced house in West Ham to look for him. We were not armed with guns. At the house, I saw that the front door was partly open. A quick search inside revealed that no one was at home. We concluded that the occupant had left quickly with some possessions.

No one at the pub was willing to help us with our investigations. There was a code of silence. However, it was established that the suspect for the murder had fled to Spain. He was extradited from Spain to this country. I think this was the first extradition from Spain and was made possible by recent legislation. However, no witnesses were willing to give evidence, and the case was dropped at court.

A public house situated in Stratford opened at 6 am for nearby market traders. It was known by everyone as 'the early house'. I went there once for a quick pint after hectic night duty. The landlord had an interesting house rule: no women were allowed on the premises. Occasionally, a couple of women would appear just after opening time to challenge this rule. The landlord would then politely escort them off the premises. Times have changed.

Reports of domestic violence were reported from time to time. There were no specialist police units at that time, and each reported crime was allocated to an available detective. I dealt with a case that typified the difficulties and frustrations we faced. A woman had been punched in the face several times by her boyfriend, causing severe bruising and cuts. As was usual, I arranged for her injuries to be photographed to preserve evidence and be available for court purposes. The photos were shocking.

I arrested her boyfriend regarding the assaults and interviewed him. He was totally unconcerned about her injuries. As an admission, he stated that he only gave her a 'dig'. The word 'dig' could be interpreted as something that she deserved, rather like a stab in the leg for an infringement of acceptable criminal behaviour.

At court, both were sat at the back of the court, snuggled up together and holding hands. The case was dropped as she did not want to go ahead with prosecuting her boyfriend.

Muggings were a problem all around London, and West Ham was no exception. They are difficult to investigate as few clues are ever available and everything relies on the victim's description of the muggers. I would try to identify the muggers by taking the victim out in a CID car for a drive around the locality to see if the victim could spot the muggers in the street. Only on one occasion was I successful. A woman had been mugged at knife point and her jewellery stolen. The next evening, I drove her around Stratford. After about twenty minutes, she spotted him. He was found guilty at court, but as he was only fifteen years old, so the punishment was very minor. She never got her jewellery back.

My posting to West Ham CID had created unbelievable challenges for me. I had survived mentally but knew that I would be linked to the episode of corruption throughout the rest of my police service. How would I be received and perceived by my future colleagues? Would I be resilient enough to cope?

I must add that other than the corruption episode, West Ham had been a marvellous introduction to front-line CID work. I had worked with outstanding detectives under the most trying of circumstances. Perhaps it was the camaraderie brought about through facing the daily hardships and challenges we confronted together.

Uniform Sergeant Barnet Police Station 1988–89

By August 1988, it was time for a temporary change in my career. I had passed the sergeants' promotion exam back in 1984 and had delayed my promotion for four years to gain CID experience. It was now time for me to become a uniform sergeant for at least a year. It was necessary to return to uniform in this rank before I could become a detective sergeant. These were the rules at the time, but all this has since changed.

Where would I be posted? It was seen as best to take promotion and serve at another police station, and there was some sense in this approach. I asked for a posting at nearby East Ham Police Station. With no logic, I was posted to Barnet instead. Barnet? Where was that? I had to look it up on the map to find it. It was on the northern border of the Met and adjoined with Hertfordshire Constabulary. Why had I been posted far, far away to this backwater? Was it punishment?

Here's a quick word about being a uniform sergeant: it involved wearing a uniform, of course, and supervising police constables. There was a wider supervisory gulf between sergeants and constables in the uniform world. Sergeants were never to be addressed by their first name by constables. I think this distance made supervision easier in a way. Additionally, most constables were in their two-year probationary period and had to be watched diligently.

The shifts were split equally between an eight-hour night duty, followed by an eight-hour day duty and an eight-hour evening duty. This meant there were as many officers on duty at 4 am when all was quiet as were on duty at 4 pm when all was busy. This was a senseless allocation of resources. Shift times have changed since then and have become more practical.

I was given no real training for this new role. I had attended a two-week training course at Hendon Police College, but it provided no practical input. The course was structured for uniform police constables transitioning to a supervisory role and didn't explain how to fill in a custody record for a prisoner. That was all I wanted to know – just the basic practical aspects of paperwork. When at West Ham, I had originally intended to spend a day or two with a custody sergeant learning the basics. It was a good plan, but there was so much do in the CID office every day that I never found the time.

My main responsibility was to be a custody sergeant. This involved booking in arrests and supervising their detention. For this role, I may as well have been a civilian: no police work was involved, and I was forbidden to investigate. I had to be impartial. It was tedious and unfulfilling. In other words, dull and boring. Frustratingly, a CID officer would sometimes approach me in the custody suite to tell me they were nipping out for a quick pint while waiting for a solicitor to attend and provide legal advice to their prisoner. How I wished I could join them!

By chance, my first shift was as a custody sergeant. I arrived early and changed into my uniform in the locker room situated in the basement. I had no desk. Wearing a uniform for the first time in over six years felt more than a little strange. I polished my shoes and asked another sergeant where the custody suite was. I walked up the stairs to my new role. The custody suite was quite busy. The custody sergeant didn't recognise me, of course, but he didn't care as I was taking over from his duties, and he was keen to go. He mumbled something about the current state of play as a handover and disappeared – probably to the pub.

My eight-hour evening shift would end at 11 pm. Back then, the pubs shut at 11 pm on the dot. Usually, the night duty sergeant would arrive ten minutes early for a quick briefing from me. I would then sprint to the nearest pub in the high street and line up a couple of pints moments before they closed. Those perfect pints kept me sane.

Most of my time as a custody sergeant was boring. When I say most, I would say 80%. To relieve the monotony, I would sketch cartoons of vintage biplanes on the white boards in the custody suite. Criminals and their solicitors would gaze at these cartoons with an air of confusion while I performed the serious business recording their detention. Fellow sergeants would often leave the cartoons intact when they took over my shift.

Barnet was fine as a posting if you liked tranquillity. Riders on horseback would wave and say hello. People were very friendly. Crime was exceedingly low compared to West Ham.

I had taken with me from West Ham about forty of days off that were owed to me. As I hated the pointless night duties, I took my first two weeks of night duty off as leave; there were enough sergeants on the shift available to cover for me. This did not please the chief superintendent. He called me to his office and told me that I was not to take any night duties off in the future. He said it was part of my development to work nights. I responded that I was entitled to take time off. He said it was unfair on the other sergeants. I said I had cleared it with the other sergeants, and there was enough to provide cover in my absence. He then played his ace card – the 'threat' card. He told me that if I continued to take night duties off as leave, he would prevent my return to the CID as a detective sergeant. This was an unfair threat, and he had no authority to enforce it. I ignored him and continued to take night duties off as and when it suited me.

I had also taken with me from West Ham a short fuse regarding anti-social behaviour. I had no time for drunken yobs, whatever their age. I consumed perhaps more beer than I should on occasion, but I never became unpleasant or sought a fight with strangers.

One evening while out and about in a car supervising police constables, I heard a call to a disturbance in a pub on the A1. I was some distance away but decided to attend. I arrived to find five men in their twenties at the bar, drunk and being offensive. The pub was mainly a restaurant, and families with children were sat at tables nearby. Six police officers had arrived before me, but the problems these drunks caused had not been resolved. I politely asked the drunks to leave. They didn't move at first, and one smashed his beer glass on the floor. I think they noticed my disapproval and they all gradually left the premises and gathered in the car park. At this point, they became rowdy and abusive, and they smashed more beer glasses. There was no reaction from the police officers gathered nearby who had almost become passive onlookers.

By now, I'd had enough; my fuse had burnt out. I told the loudest drunk that I was arresting him for being drunk and disorderly. Two officers took hold of him and led him to the police van parked nearby. At this point, one of the other drunks objected and started swearing at me, saying there was no way his mate should be arrested. I could see that families with young children nearby were shocked. I arrested him for also being drunk and disorderly. Guess what happened next? The remaining three drunks did the same, and I also arrested them. They ended up sitting together in the police van to Barnet Police Station. There was some surprise in the custody suite when I alone was the arresting officer for all five. They all pleaded guilty at court and received fines. It was a small victory for justice. Was I overzealous in my actions? I don't think so. There are times when you must be firm and unyielding in the police. Drunken yobs do not respect conciliation and prevarication; they instinctively see it as weakness. These yobs had every opportunity to disperse quietly into the night, but they chose confrontation with me. Also, I think I provided an example to the other officers on how to deal with such situations. Most of them were young probationers and only in their first year or two of police service.

Barnet football club had a very loyal fan base, and their ground used to be within walking distance of Barnet Police Station. For home matches, Barnet police used to send a uniform sergeant and six police constables to police the ground. Several times I had the job of walking with my constables from Barnet Police Station down the slope of the Great North Road and to the ground on the right-hand side. Back then, Barnet FC was struggling financially to survive. Stan Flashman had joined them as manager in 1985 and was in the process of saving them. He was a controversial character to say the least. The team achieved promotion in 1991 thanks to his efforts. He had the habit of straying onto the pitch in excitement during the game and winding up the visiting supporters. I could have made quite a name for myself by arresting him for that! But, the tea supplied to us during the match by Barnet FC was of such excellent quality that it would have been so unfair to arrest him. I had my standards!

I remember one incident that year – a pub fight. Police officers rarely encounter them. They are usually over very quickly, and by the time the police arrive, all will be found to be quiet. One evening at about 8 pm, I was parked opposite a pub in East Barnet. Sat with me was a new police constable. I always preferred to sit and watch what was happening on the streets rather than drive around aimlessly. Suddenly, half a dozen people spilled out of the front door of the pub, fighting with each other. More exited the pub to continue the fight. Before we stepped out of the car, I made a radio call asking for assistance and describing the situation in brief. This was not a time to rush in; with only two of us, it was best to approach calmly and try to subdue the situation while help arrived. I indicated to the new police officer to hang back and not rush in. I also instructed him to stick to me like glue for his own protection.

By the time we had crossed the road, there were at least twenty men and a few women grabbing and punching each other. Thankfully, none of them turned on us. We pushed through the melee to see if anyone in the pub had been seriously injured but encountered even more fighting. There were calls on the radio asking if we were okay and to tell us that help was on the way. I requested that the police units continue to make their way as we were outnumbered and facing an uncertain future.

Very shortly afterwards, I heard sirens, and eight officers jumped from a van to intervene and calm things down. By now, most had stopped fighting, but a few refused to do so and were arrested for public disorder. There were no serious injuries to anyone. What caused it all? I have no idea. No doubt the quantities of beer drunk sparked a grievance from long ago. Having tried at West Ham to take written statements from pub-goers the day after a stabbing incident, I quickly learnt that memory soaked in alcohol is the first casualty of a pub fight.

One afternoon, I was on patrol on my own in a police car. At about 1 pm, a call came over the radio from the control room at New Scotland Yard that an armed robbery was taking place at a building society nearby on Darkes Lane, Potters Bar. By an amazing coincidence, this was only about three hundred yards away from me. I notified the controller that I would attend. At speed, I raced to the building society and pulled up outside. I ran to the door carrying my wooden truncheon – I didn't want to face a shotgun without a defensive weapon! I carefully opened the door, but there were no robbers inside. A cashier shouted to me that they had just that second run off down the adjacent alley. I turned and ran down the alley but could not find them; they had probably made off in a waiting car. Without considering the consequences, I had put my life in danger. There are not many countries where an unarmed police officer would hurry to confront armed robbers, but it often happens here.

I think the only benefit Barnet offered me was that there was no mention by anyone of my recent action against corruption. Perhaps they were unaware of it – I certainly didn't mention it.

I recall no other incidents of note while at Barnet, although I do recall that I was second in charge of Barnet's Lost Dog Book. I had no paperwork to worry about. Everything was handed over to the next shift. As a detective, I had piles of files on my desk. There was no one to hand them over to. It was all down to me, to use a police expression. Only I could spin those plates.

I was there for a year before being nominated to return to the CID as a detective sergeant in October 1989. I learned little new while at

Barnet and, if anything, I became deskilled as a detective. The interchange system of sending detectives back to uniform as part of the promotion system was scrapped soon afterwards. I was lucky to only spend a year on the interchange system – many were away from the CID for five years or more. A few decided to stay in their uniform posting as it provided a predictable life and without the sudden imposition of extra duties when serious crimes occurred.

Detective Sergeant Tottenham CID 1989–91

My next posting was as a detective sergeant. It was a case of out of the frying pan of West Ham and into the fire of Tottenham. This was a police station that was still very conscious of the murder of PC Blakelock at the Broadwater Farm in October 1985, just four years previously. My joining instructions included a safety booklet on the Broadwater Farm. The booklet strongly advised that I should always have an exit route in mind from the Broadwater Farm Estate ready should I ever need to leave quickly. Not a very encouraging start! I was to be at Tottenham from October 1989 to October 1991.

In essence, a detective sergeant supervises detective constables and has a role in investigating more complex and sensitive crimes. It is often regarded as being the best rank in the Met. A detective sergeant is slightly removed from the frequent drudgery of the coal face yet is free from desk-bound managerial commitments. They are also an accepted part of the general CID office camaraderie, whereas a detective inspector is not. The detective sergeant's supervisory relationship with detective constables is far more blurred than between uniform constables and uniform sergeants. For one, detective constables are on first-name terms with their detective sergeants. There is a practical reason for this. At times, both will be working together in a covert capacity, and it would be detrimental to the operation if the word 'sergeant' was used. This familiarity can, of course, weaken the supervisory role of the detective sergeant and make the job harder if they take a disciplinary stance against a detective constable. The supervisory relationship between a uniform sergeant and a uniform police constable is easier to define, and first name terms are certainly not acceptable.

To my eyes, the Broadwater Farm estate resembled a gigantic alien spaceship that had crash-landed in the middle of a 1930s housing estate sometime during the 1970s. It was made of concrete slabs, and all the housing blocks were built on stilts to protect from local flooding. All the housing blocks were connected by walkways above ground. About five thousand council residents lived there. There was a dedicated group of police officers assigned to the estate and were known as the Broadwater Farm Unit (BFU). They were housed in a portacabin in the station yard.

Tottenham was far more multi-cultural than West Ham. Somehow, they all seemed to get along together without too much friction. To this day, I believe that police officers take people as they find them and are probably more open-minded than most of the public. Police officers meet all sections of the community as part of their job and have a more balanced view from this experience. I found abundant racism between various ethnic groups on a scale and intensity that would shock the public.

Tottenham Police Station was a Victorian building and far too small for the modern age. There had been some extending vertically by adding an extra floor, but this was not enough. The basic design was a square with a small yard for parking in the middle, known as the station yard. To complicate matters, a police horse stable was part of the premises.

These stables have now long since gone, but by 1989, they were famous for their Christmas parties. In some place or other, an evil concoction of something called 'beer' was brewed during the year in time for the Christmas party. This 'beer' was very dark in colour and rumoured to have started life as discarded diesel engine sump oil. Whatever the recipe, it was strong and tasty. These parties were hilarious for many reasons; I think they helped let off steam and were good for morale. Inevitably, as the police became more precious about their public image, these Christmas parties were banned. Instead, we just went elsewhere.

I was an acting detective inspector in my last year at Tottenham.

Tottenham CID was not the same as West Ham CID. Tottenham CID management, comprising a detective chief inspector and two detective inspectors, held different attitudes compared to their opposite numbers at West Ham. There was a puritanical management atmosphere at Tottenham: all three CID managers refrained from joining their detectives for a beer after work. A few scotches in the office on a Friday afternoon would be unthinkable. One of the DIs used to go for a long run every lunchtime. This would have been unheard of in the past. I think the puritan attitude was management's attempt to distance themselves from the more hedonistic times of the '70s and '80s. Having said that, the DCI was highly experienced and very fair towards us, although I think he found my humour trying at times. He did once remark that he thought I was very resilient without saying why.

Tottenham and West Ham CID were otherwise similar. Both were understaffed, under-resourced, and swamped with work. Tottenham, however, had a world-famous football team, which brought its own policing problems. Match days were not a problem for the CID as it was almost purely a concern for uniform officers. Visiting fans mainly arrived at Seven Sisters tube station and walked up High Road to the ground. On a match day, the fast-food outlets lining the road would take more money in a day than they would in a month.

The people of Tottenham suffered far more muggings than those of West Ham. This was a crime that was always difficult to solve. The shock of being threatened at knife point and faced by a small crowd of muggers confuses the memory. Furthermore, the muggers would swap clothing and make off in different directions. The vast majority doing this were youths – a tiny fraction of all youths in the Tottenham area. It was quite possible that only one in a thousand youths in Tottenham carried out these muggings, but their crimes negatively impacted community relations. The majority of those mugged were people returning home from work or going about their business during the day – certainly not gang members.

These muggings could amount to over twenty a day. As a detective, I came to know the names of many of these muggers, who often had a history of such crime. They were on the street, gathering in gangs constantly from about 2 pm until the small hours. The gangs would be from five to twenty youths. The muggings were not planned but spontaneous. Passers-by would not know that a mugging was taking place. The gang would carefully surround their victim and ensured that only the victim saw the blade.

Another mugging method was called 'steaming'. A crowd of youths would swarm into a shop and ransack it in minutes. The staff would be too fearful to intervene, and the muggers would be gone before the police arrived. Muggers employed similar methods on buses.

For much of my two-year posting at Tottenham, I managed the CID burglary investigation unit. This unit was situated in the main CID office. Me, five detective constables, and three uniform officers working in plain clothes made up the unit. At that time, about fifteen burglaries were committed daily in the Tottenham area. As is usual in the police, the seven officers assigned were very rarely all available to investigate burglaries. Every day, officers would find themselves with other commitments, such as court appearances, training courses, and annual leave. Of the eight officers, it was normal to have only four available for a burglary investigation. Additionally, we were viewed as a standby source of officers should a high-profile incident occur. The following is one such example.

In 1990, a murder was committed at a nightclub opposite Tottenham Police Station in Tottenham High Road. A young man was stabbed with a knife and died at the scene. A murder team of detectives attended Tottenham Police Station to investigate the murder. Within a day, a man was charged. At that time in the Metropolitan Police Service, the murder investigation process dictated that, after someone had been charged with murder, it would then be investigated by local detectives at the police station. This posed a problem: we had no spare detectives. I was leading the burglary team, which was deluged with work. However, it was decided that my team would now be responsible for the ongoing investigation. There would be no choice but to slim down our burglary investigations and divert our energies to the murder investigation. The investigation was complicated in that detectives had to speak to the hundreds attending the club to ascertain if they had seen the murder or could provide information. In addition, all their names and addresses, clothing descriptions, and statements had to be written on cards and cross-referenced. There were no officers available to assist us with this, and there were no police computers available.

I decided that the only option was to ask my family to help. My wife and teenage son assisted by completing these cards at my home. This was of great help. They were not paid for this vital voluntary work, of course. At management meetings, the burglary unit was often criticised for not making enough arrests for burglaries and that the number of burglaries had increased. I had to explain that we were also investigating a complex murder at the same time. I began to realise that it was often the role of senior police management to complain rather than praise. Senior management was composed of career uniform officers who had no experience of CID work and found it easy to take cheap pot shots at us.

Around this time, a member of the IRA was arrested in Lordship Lane, Tottenham. It occurred during the early hours of the morning. Two uniform officers in a police car became suspicious and tried to stop the car. A short high-speed chase followed, after which the driver ran off. He was chased and caught by the officers, who were unarmed. Inside the boot of the car were two machine guns, ammunition, and a spade. The guns and spade were covered in soil. It turned out that the driver was a member of the IRA and just prior to his arrest had apparently dug up the guns from their hiding place. He was charged by the Anti-Terrorist Branch at New Scotland Yard with terrorism offences. At the Old Bailey, his defence was that he did not know the guns were in the boot and that the car belonged to a distant relative. The jury believed him, and he was freed. On the 16th February 1992, he and other members of the IRA attacked a police station in Northern Ireland with a heavy machine gun and other weapons. He and all the IRA team were ambushed and killed by SAS soldiers.

A female police officer was seconded to us for about six months as part of her accelerated promotion process. She was a university graduate accepted by the National Police College in Bramshill, Hampshire, since she was suitable for fast progress through the ranks. At this time, she'd had about a year in the police. She would have achieved the rank of inspector within five years. This would normally take about ten years at least. She went on to achieve the rank of deputy assistant commissioner when I last checked at the time of writing this book. She was one of the few women in the police that I had any time for and was a good choice for promotion by the powers that were.

She was on duty with me one evening, and a request was made to attend the scene of an attempted poisoning of a husband by his wife. We arrived at the house and discovered that the uniform WPC who was first on the scene had thrown the poison down the kitchen sink, thus destroying crucial evidence. It transpired that the situation was complex: over time, the husband had become very severely disabled, and his wife had found life impossible to cope with. There had been apparently no help from social services. In fairness, social services were, of course, also deluged with work. The wife had not actually given him any poison. In my view, her actions were more of a cry for help. I therefore decided to abuse the criminal justice system for her benefit. I arrested her for attempting to poison her husband. I knew this arrest would not result in a prosecution, but it was a means to an end. With the wife taken away to the police station, social services had no choice but to take her husband away to a place of care. My actions gave the wife a welcome relief from her gruelling predicament and ensured that her husband now had the assistance of social services. CID investigations could be unusually complex at times and required innovative action.

In general, the court process was frustrating both to the public and the police. It always appeared to favour the criminal. A criminal at court was always supported by a solicitor and often a social worker and other support agencies. The member of the public who had volunteered to give evidence publicly against the criminal had no such support. There wasn't even a separate waiting room for witnesses; instead, they had to wait for hours in a public area with the criminals awaiting their trial. This experience did not encourage witnesses to come forward and help the police in the future.

I also found the court system to be frustrating. Here is an example. After a long day at work, I was off duty and walking towards my parked car. A fast-food van was parked nearby, where kebabs and chips were being sold. A youth next to the van was shouting and screaming at the seller and causing a disturbance. He was also swearing loudly. I approached and asked him to behave himself. He then started banging on the van with his fist, growing even more agitated. I arrested him for public disorder and took him to Tottenham Police Station. He appeared some months later at the Young Offenders Magistrate's Court in Highgate. I was required to give evidence against him as he denied the charge.

As was normal, I had made a written note of the incident in my police pocketbook just after his arrest, outlining his behaviour and the words he had used. Due to the time lapse, I asked to refer to my official pocketbook for evidence. As I did so, the magistrate slammed down his pen and told the court that he was "sick and tired of police officers reading from their pocketbook when giving evidence". I closed my pocketbook and put it to one side. The magistrate then asked me to continue with my evidence without the pocketbook. I stood still and said nothing. After a long pause, he demanded to know why I was silent. I told him that I could not remember the details as it was so long ago and, in fairness to the court, I did not want to get any details wrong. There was another pause. The magistrate changed his mind and said that I could now refer to my notes.

I found this incident to be typical of the way police officers were often treated by magistrates and lawyers. It was humiliating; I had made an off-duty arrest when I could have just walked on by. I had also put myself at risk of physical harm. Here was this magistrate living in his 'ivory tower', treating me as if I was a lowlife. It was as if criminals were treated with far more courtesy than police officers. Perhaps as a disciplined force, we police were reluctant to challenge their behaviour?

A 'sting' shop was set up in the heart of

Tottenham to catch out thieves and muggers trying to sell on stolen items. The shop was staffed by undercover police officers based at New Scotland Yard and unknown to the local criminals. The shop advertised that it would buy jewellery and electrical goods. It had covert video cameras and audio devices to record the criminals when they made a sale. They were asked to sign a disclaimer form, which recorded their fingerprints. The officers at Tottenham were not told about this shop to ensure that secrecy would be maintained. The shop became so successful in gathering evidence that the CID became aware of its activity. One detective, along with a colleague, decided that he would pay them a visit to give the staff there a piece of his mind. They both went into the shop, where he lectured the staff, telling them that their behaviour was disgraceful and that they had to stop buying stolen goods; otherwise, there would be trouble. All this was recorded on the video system. He never lived it down and was reminded of it continually.

Not long after this, I went with a colleague to meet with the legal representative of a burglar arrested earlier that day. I walked into the custody area of Tottenham Police Station, and the custody sergeant indicated to me where the legal representative was sitting. I recognised this legal representative as the corrupt detective sergeant I had gathered covert evidence against back in 1986 when I was at West Ham. He was not a qualified solicitor but was there simply to provide legal advice to the burglar and be present during the interview. We recognised each other, but nothing was said between us. I walked out of the custody suite. Obviously, I decided that another officer should take my place for this investigation.

At about this time, a block of private flats was being built opposite Tottenham Police Station. One colleague commented that they would be for either villains or more victims of crime. This comment rather typified our perspective of the population.

One criminal was regularly arrested and brought to Tottenham for offences such as assault. He had been arrested in connection with the murder of PC Blakelock a few years earlier. He was known to have been involved, but it could not be proved. Whenever he was arrested and brought into the police station, he would say to the custody sergeant, "Your head on the end of a pole next!" I was always amazed at the tolerance and patience of police officers not to react to this incitement.

I arrested a suspected gang rapist who was part of a crime family in Tottenham. I went to see him in his cell to tell him that his solicitor was on his way. As I opened the cell door to speak to him, he stood, undid his trousers, and urinated on the floor in front of me. Unfortunately, the victim of the rape did not pick him out in an identity parade as one of the rapists, and he had to be released. There was no other evidence against him other than a close physical description, including scars to the face.

I investigated a particular mugging that was to cause me some frustration with the CPS. A woman was waiting at a bus stop when three youths approached and, using force against her, stole her handbag. They ran off into a nearby car and drove off. The woman wrote the number of the car down on a piece of paper. She reported this to the police. About thirty minutes later, the car was spotted by police officers and stopped. The men in the car matched the description of the muggers the woman had provided. All three men were arrested. The car was searched, but there was no trace of the handbag or contents. All three denied any involvement in the mugging. They told us about ten minutes before the police stopped them that they had bought the car from a man in a pub but did not know his name. I arranged for identity parades to be held, but the woman failed to pick them out in the line ups. The CPS refused to support a criminal prosecution, and the men were released. The CPS view was that there was insufficient evidence to connect the men with the muggings. I disagreed and felt that the seriousness of the offence justified a court appearance. The difficulty for the CPS is that they require at least a 51% certainty of conviction at court before they proceed. I've never understood how this 51% can be empirically measured. In essence, I think it means a likelihood that the muggers would have been found guilty by a jury. The CPS must meet government targets. If a case fails at court, it counts against the CPS as a performance failure. Before the days of the CPS, the CID would certainly have charged these muggers and hoped the jury would convict them. If they were not convicted, the police view would have been 'they'll come again'. This meant they were certain to be arrested again for something else.

I was called to a sad and disturbing incident one winter morning. An elderly woman had been found dead in her small, terraced house. She was lying on the floor and had a few bruises to her face and body. It was initially thought that she had been assaulted and murdered. However, it was established that the low temperature in her home had caused her to suffer from hypothermia. This condition caused her to become disorientated and confused. She would have bumped into the doors, walls, and furniture, causing bruises. She was killed by the cold. She obviously could not afford to heat her home.

A particularly violent incident occurred in 1991. A schoolteacher was asleep at night in his bed. He was alone and lived in a three-bedroom terraced house near Bruce Grove in Tottenham. At about midnight, he was woken in his bed by an intruder standing over him and demanding to know "where the women" were. This man was over six feet tall and well built. There were no women in the house, and the teacher tried to explain this to the intruder. Without warning, the teacher was then repeatedly stabbed in the body and neck with a large carving knife as he lay in bed. He was stabbed with such ferocity that the knife blade bent. The teacher was also struck over the head with a television and a steam iron. The teacher rightly believed that he would die if he stayed in bed which was now saturated in blood.

The attacker then went to the next bedroom, possibly to look for women. The teacher seized this opportunity and ran from his bedroom and down the stairs to escape. As he ran, blood spurted from his neck along the wall. He reached the front door, but it was bolted and chained. As he fumbled with the lock and chain, he heard his attacker scream out to him at the top of the stairs. He managed to open the door just as the attacker flew down the stairs towards him. The teacher ran out into the deserted street. Luck was now on his side: a police patrol car was passing. The police car happened to be there because a group of muggers who were supposed to be at home during a court-imposed curfew had been spotted in a street nearby by the officer. The officer immediately rushed to help the teacher and saved his live by applying pressure to the neck wound with his uniform cap. Meanwhile, the attacker had escaped.

I commenced duty at 8 am the next morning and took charge of the investigation. The attacker had to be found as quickly as possible before he struck again. He obviously had murderous intent and was also a severe danger to women.

Although this clearly was a case of attempted murder, no assistance was available from murder squad officers as the teacher had not yet died. However, the first twenty-four hours of a murder investigation are critical for securing evidence and building an evidential case. It was left to me and my small burglary team to do this vital work.

The teacher's house was forensically examined and photographed. I did not enter the house as I wanted to preserve the scene forensically. However, the photographs revealed a very disturbing crime scene. I had never seen so much blood. The bed was almost all red in colour, and the mattress was soaked in blood. There were blood spurts from the teacher's neck wound as he had descended the stairs. The carving knife had been taken from the kitchen draw and left behind by the attacker. The blade was bent and covered in blood.

There was no sign of forced entry to the house on the ground floor. The windows were secure, as was the back door. The front door was obviously locked as the teacher had to unlock it and remove the security chain to make good his escape from the attacker. So, how did the attacker get in?

It had been a warm evening, and the teacher had left his bedroom window open. This window overlooked the street. The forensic examiner had found a shoe print on a chair positioned underneath the bedroom window. This shoe print had a training shoe pattern. It did not match any that the teacher owned. It was safe to assume that the attacker had climbed the drainpipe at the front of the house to gain entry through the open window. Shoe prints can be as unique as fingerprints: once a shoe has been worn, the owner's use causes different patterns of scuffs and wear to appear on the soles. We now had a vital piece of potential forensic evidence.

Significantly, a fingerprint was found in a blood stain on the bedroom wall. Fingerprints can last for a hundred years, but this one had obviously been made during the attack. It did not match the teacher's fingerprints. We now had our second piece of potential forensic evidence.

The fingerprint experts at New Scotland Yard now applied their expertise to identify the attacker from the fingerprint found in the blood. With speed and precision, they identified him. He was a well-known Tottenham criminal with a string of convictions for violence. At the time of this attack, he was on licence from prison. Several years earlier, he had been convicted of stabbing a man in the throat. It had been a random attack in a Tottenham cafe. The man was elderly and seated at a table on his own; he was lucky to survive. The attacker had also been arrested six years earlier for his suspected part in the murder of PC Keith Blakelock on the Broadwater Farm. However, he was not convicted of PC Blakelock's murder.

We established where the attacker lived in Tottenham; it was only a few streets away from where the teacher lived and was also a terraced house of Victorian design. I decided we would visit his address at 6 am and hopefully have a chance of finding him indoors. There were three of us plus a police dog handler I had requested. The presence of a police dog always has a calming influence on violent criminals! These were different times to today – we did not have body armour, sprays, or tasers. Today, officers will use guns due to the risk to life the attacker posed.

One officer went to the rear of the house to let us know if he tried to escape. I rang the doorbell. Shortly afterwards, a man matching the attacker's description opened the door. He appeared to be calm. I told him who we were and showed him identification. He told us his name; we had the right man. I arrested him for attempted murder, and he was handcuffed. He denied any knowledge of the stabbing. We searched the house and found a pair of training shoes in his bedroom that appeared to match the footprint found on the chair in the teacher's bedroom. No drugs or weapons were found. Throughout all this, the attacker was calm and said little other than to deny the attack. He did not threaten us. He was taken to Tottenham Police Station and booked in with the custody sergeant.

I interviewed him at Tottenham Police Station in the presence of his solicitor. He repeated his denial that he had any involvement in the attack and said he had no memory of the evening in question. He was charged with attempted murder and remained in prison until his trial some months later at the Old Bailey. He was found guilty by the court and sentenced to a lengthy imprisonment term.

The teacher who was attacked used to shave with a razor but changed to an electric one after the attack. He could no longer face having a metal blade at his throat. Quite understandable, I think.

Rape is justifiably regarded as a serious crime and as much so when I was at Tottenham. However, the truth can be very elusive in many rape investigations. The following is an example.

A fourteen-year-old girl living with her family in Tottenham went missing one night. She returned home to her worried family in the morning and told them that she had been kidnapped and repeatedly raped by different men while she was tied to a tree in the back garden of a drinking club. The club was situated in Tottenham High Road; a terraced house with a garden at the rear, overlooked by residential houses on either side. The girl's clothes were not damaged or stained. The girl could not account for how she had been taken to the rear garden. It appeared to me that she had concocted this story to cover staying overnight with friends and did not want to get into trouble with her parents.

In the presence of her mother, I challenged the girl about the veracity of her account. She admitted that she had stayed at a friend's house and did not want to get into trouble for doing so. Her mother had provided the girl with a protective upbringing and would not have allowed her to stay anywhere overnight. The investigation, therefore, came to an end, and a huge amount of police time was saved. The reason I mention this incident is that today, I would be severely criticised for the action I took to establish the truth by challenging the girl's account. Today, any person who tells the police that they have been raped must be believed whatever the circumstances. This, of course, leads to a massive waste of police time if the allegation is false. It can also lead to the arrest of innocent people.

There has always been criticism of the low conviction rate for rape. The feminist view is that the police are institutionally sexist, deliberately fail to investigate rapes, and never take the victim's account seriously. This view is wrong, malicious, and destructive: specialist rape investigation units have a high proportion of female detectives particularly determined to bring offenders to justice. However, rapes are rarely as clear-cut as the public expects. Most reported rapes are from women about their partners either in the recent past or very distant past. Inevitably, there are no witnesses, and forensic evidence is almost worthless as both have or had an ongoing relationship. As mentioned, the CPS must meet a 51% chance of a successful prosecution threshold. In essence, there is insufficient evidence to meet this threshold in most of these cases. There is a minimum imprisonment of seven years upon conviction for rape. With weak prosecution cases, juries are reluctant to find the accused guilty if he is to face a minimum of seven years in prison.

Death by drowning was a rare event in Tottenham. An unusual drowning that proved to be the exception occurred in the River Lea, which ran through Tottenham from north to south before joining the River Thames. A lock at Ferry Lane was manually operated by barge and boat crews as they navigated along the river. Surrounding the lock were light industrial units. One afternoon, Tottenham police received a call from a member of the public that a body was floating in the lock. It transpired to be a male in his thirties who had been in the water for several days. The post-mortem concluded that the deceased had drowned, and there were no suspicious circumstances. He was identified as having lived nearby and a building labourer by trade. He was unmarried, a non-swimmer, and an unlikely suicide victim.

I decided to try to establish the circumstances of his death. The last time he was seen alive was at an Irish dance hall in Holloway the previous Friday evening. At about midnight, he was seen getting into a minicab alone outside the dance hall. As a result of my observations outside the dance hall on a Friday evening, I managed to identify the mini-cab driver. I interviewed him, and he recalled running the victim to Ferry Lane adjacent to the lock. The fare was paid, but the driver did not see in which direction the passenger had headed. The passenger should have crossed Ferry Lane to go home on the adjacent housing estate. Instead, he must have headed in the opposite direction towards the lock area. To walk to the lock area from the minicab would have involved him travelling a short distance along the pavement and then descending a flight of stairs. Overhead lights clearly illuminated this area. He would then have had to approach the edge of the lock by walking a few more yards and enter the water. As I mentioned, he was a non-swimmer. He had lived in this area for some time, and I could not see how he could have taken this route by mistake. He had drunk a few beers that night but, in my opinion, not enough to confuse his sense of direction.

Had the minicab driver murdered him by pushing him into the water after stealing his cash? He could possibly have been thrown over the wall from Ferry Lane and into the lock. The cab driver was strongly built. CCTV was not present, and there were no witnesses. We will never know. Despite best efforts, not all investigations are conclusive.

I now had ten years of police service and had probably crammed more experience into those years than 95% of police officers. Could my police life become even more intense and demanding? I was about to find out the answer to this question.

Detective Sergeant 'The Flying Squad' Rigg Approach 1991–92

In 1991, I decided to apply for a posting to the Flying Squad. The police term back then for the Flying Squad was SO8 (Specialist Operations 8). I reasoned that my ten years of police experience to date had been limited to routine CID work and that the time had come to specialise. The Flying Squad's main role was to arrest armed bank robbers and those involved in armed robberies of cash in transit vans such as Securicor and jewellers. The Flying Squad had four departments around London. The nearest to me was at a road named Rigg Approach in Leytonstone, East London. Its office was above an empty set of garages on an industrial estate. The office was therefore known as Rigg Approach – a name that, in time, would become nationally infamous for organised police corruption.

My written application for the Flying Squad was accepted, and I was invited to attend an interview at New Scotland Yard. It went well, and I passed the selection, receiving notification that I would start at Rigg Approach on October 1991. There was some surprise among my colleagues that I had been accepted, as they thought the Flying Squad culture at that time would not readily accept a 'grass' such as me. Of note, by the time I left Tottenham, I was an acting detective inspector.

The Flying Squad had become famous through the 1970s television series *The Sweeney*, starring John Thaw and Denis Waterman. This series failed to accurately represent the day-to-day life of a Flying Squad detective. It did, however, create a degree of glamour to the role. There were detectives on the Flying Squad who modelled themselves on Reagan and Carter in their manners of speech and actions. Was this a case of life imitating art?

I now left the relative certainty and security of life within Tottenham CID to begin the next chapter of my career. I no longer held the rank of acting detective inspector as my new posting was for detective sergeant. It was supposed to be a posting of four years.

On my first day, I parked my car in a small car park opposite a bland concrete building in an equally bland industrial estate. This building was the Flying Squad office, 'Rigg Approach'. As I gathered my belongings from my car, I noticed several faces at the office windows. I had obviously been spotted. Was I some sort of police celebrity? I wondered. I crossed the road and pressed the security button on the ground floor's main door. I was now unknowingly about to commence the worst year of my life.

The Flying Squad at that time had four departments around London. There was 'Rigg Approach' in the northeast, Tower Bridge in the southeast, Finchley in the northwest, and Barnes in southwest London. There was an administrative HQ at New Scotland Yard presided over by a commander. The rank of commander was unique to the Met and was equivalent to assistant chief constable.

The Flying Squad at Rigg Approach was often described by its own detectives as a 'big boys' crime squad'. I had almost come full circle from my days seven years earlier on the crime squad at Wanstead, where I had been a keen embryonic detective.

'Rigg', as it was known on the Flying Squad, was isolated from everyday uniform police contact and was almost an independent outpost from the Metropolitan Police. There was no uniform police station attached to the Rigg Approach building; Rigg had its own hierarchy and culture. The other three Flying Squad offices within the Metropolitan Police area were physically attached to police stations. This lack of physical attachment to a police station with uniform officers of superior rank was to create unfortunate disparities of rank within Rigg, which ultimately became ruled by personality rather than ability and rank.

I will explain more fully. When I joined Rigg, the detective chief inspector (DCI) in post was an honest and accomplished detective. He was the 'boss' at Rigg. He had been on my selection board, and I had known him from my days at West Ham.

Next in line to this detective chief inspector were three detective inspectors and eight detective sergeants. The rest were detective constables. There were about forty-five detectives at Rigg. A few had an additional role as our surveillance unit. I wasn't suited to a surveillance role; I was often mistaken for a police officer before I joined the police. This was probably due to my height and countenance.

Three uniform police constables also worked in plain clothes. Their unique job was to drive 'gunships'. These 'gunships' were fast, plain cars crewed with armed detectives. They were used on active surveillance operations where the arrest of armed robbers was imminent. These three officers were highly trained fast car drivers of great experience, carefully selected from many applicants for the role. One of the gunship drivers at Rigg was a PC I had worked with when I was a probationary uniform constable at Barkingside back in 1981–82. He was somewhat abrasive, but I both liked and respected him for his professional competence. In my view, he had natural leadership qualities, but like so many with this attribute in the police, he declined to seek promotion. In addition to being armed with guns, we were permitted to carry pickaxe handles if resistance was expected.

Within a couple of weeks of joining, a detective inspector asked me if I wanted a firearms training course. This would have qualified me to carry a gun on armed operations and kill if need be. I answered that I would give it some thought. My response seemed to shock him; I did not view firearms as the answer to everything. I was trained in the use of handguns and automatic weapons in the Royal Navy, and they held no macho attraction. To me, it was more important to find evidence through informants and other criminal intelligence than to rely on detectives with guns. Two women at Rigg were employed as typists. One later mentioned that she had to shower the testosterone off when she returned home. Rigg was a very macho environment.

About two months after I joined Rigg, the detective chief inspector transferred to a post elsewhere. A new DCI was brought in. At this point, life became very much more difficult for me.

This new detective chief inspector created a 'topsy-turvy' world at Rigg. The gunship drivers I mentioned now had enhanced status. The new and unofficial role of two of the drivers was to drive the DCI home in a gunship and pick him up in the morning. This allowed the new DCI to indulge in his late afternoon appointments with a bottle of scotch and without the risk of being breathalysed on his way home. It was a misuse of resources, but it provided the two drivers with enhanced status and power beyond their rank. These drivers lived in East London, but it was not their role to do this. One of the drivers became hostile towards me. His status meant that my superior rank was now almost meaningless without the support of line management, and he knew it.

Furthermore, certain detective constables had the 'ear' of the new DCI and, in effect, outranked me. There was a culture of an 'inner sanctum', which was said to have access to extra overtime payments. There were suggestions of a Masonic influence. The detective sergeant I had convicted at West Ham five years previously was a Mason, as were some of the detectives at Rigg.

I now noticed that former detectives I had previously worked with were reluctant to speak with me when other detectives were around. When no one else was around, they were friendly.

I was now in a rather strange position. I had a criminal underworld informant who provided me with regular, reliable information about armed robbers. He was an active armed robber of banks and building societies. I was the only detective to have an informant of this calibre and reliability at Rigg; informants were the key to success as they provided inside information. With it, there was no need for lengthy, expensive police surveillance operations against suspected armed robbers. An informant could tell you exactly who was not only committing armed robberies but also when their next robbery would be, where it would be, and who was involved. However, it was no easy task to manage such an informant; they'd have to trust me not to give him away – not only to the police but also to his gang. To do so could have cost him his life. Informants of this calibre were not only exceedingly difficult to find but also challenging to keep. I had achieved this through my own efforts and with help from no one.

My informant was successful. Due to his triumph in helping me arrest armed robbers, he was rewarded with £4,000 in cash at New Scotland Yard in person by David Veness, a Metropolitan Police assistant commissioner. (£4,000 in 1992 would be worth about £12,000 in 2021). I had been providing my informant with money from my own pocket for all his information. The police were never able to recompense me for that loss. For me to give money to informants from my own pocket was against police regulations, and I could have been sacked. I think it is safe to say that no chief constable has ever trodden this fine line. The risks I took as far as my liberty and career could never be rewarded with promotion; I did it for the public good.

I received a phone call from a British Transport Police constable on the evening of this £4,000 reward at New Scotland Yard. My informant had been arrested at Victoria railway station public toilets, slumped on the floor in a cubicle. A small quantity of drugs and almost £4,000 in cash were in his pockets. He had told them he was my informant and had been paid the money that day at New Scotland Yard. These officers were rather amazed when I confirmed this – but how else do you reward a criminal underworld informant other than with cash?

When dealing with this informant, I sometimes put my freedom and career at risk. I took risks to catch dangerous criminals and protect the public. As an example, I met this informant as part of an investigation into a planned armed robbery, where a loaded gun would be used. He told me that the gun was in his car parked nearby. He offered to show me the gun to substantiate his information. At this point, I should have arrested him and seized the gun. Technically, I would have failed in my duty as a police officer not to do so. However, I saw the bigger picture: to arrest a gang of armed robbers who had committed many armed robberies and would go on to commit many more and possibly kill someone along the way. Had my informant been carrying a recording device, I would have lost my job and probably have been imprisoned. I was treading a difficult line with help from no one. I could not ask for advice from a more senior officer; their advice would have been to arrest the informant. Not to do so would have implicated the more senior officer with me in a criminal offence of failing to seize the gun and arrest my informant. Was this a form of corruption I was engaged in? I don't think there is an easy answer.

The best informants are active criminals who decide to trust a police officer with information. There can be a sinister aspect to be aware of when dealing with an informant. In exchange for information, the informant may ask the detective for information that relates to the informant's criminal friends. He may ask if his friends are under police surveillance. This information can result in thousands of pounds in payment to the detective from the criminal. Suddenly, the detective becomes corrupt and at a point of no return to the straight and narrow. He is now ensnared with no hope of escape. His paymasters would, of course, blackmail him should he refuse to assist.

Here is one example of how valuable my informant was regarding the investigation of armed robberies. An armed robbery with a gun took place against a Royal Mail van in East London, and a large quantity of cash was stolen. My informant told me that the driver was involved in the crime. It was often the case that drivers and guards were involved in these crimes by providing information to the robbers about their van's route and timings. I arrested the driver. He fully admitted in a taped interview the conspiracy to steal from the Royal Mail van and was convicted at court. The investigation cost the taxpayer almost nothing thanks to my informant.

One of my investigations at Rigg followed the arrest of two robbers armed with a loaded shotgun as they attacked a security van full of cash. Two unarmed detectives from Stoke Newington Police Station happened to be driving past when they saw two masked men approach a parked security van. One of the men was holding a shotgun. The detectives stopped their car and rushed the two robbers. Their swift and brave actions resulted in the robbers being disarmed and arrested. The gun was a sawn-off shotgun, and it was loaded. With the robbers was a bag within which they had carried the gun and masks to the scene of the robbery. It became my task to investigate this armed robbery. Of interest, in Flying Squad terminology, a robber's bag containing guns and masks was known as a 'Happy Bag'. Quite why this was so, I never found out.

One of the robbers was a former security van driver; he had no previous criminal convictions. His accomplice lived in Stoke Newington and had a history of criminal offending.

Several months later, both appeared at the Old Bailey for trial. The one who had been a security van driver told the court that he had been walking past the van when for, no reason, two detectives from Stoke Newington jumped on him. This was obviously not true. At this point, his accomplice decided to turn Queen's Evidence and give evidence against his accomplice. This was a very, very unusual event in criminal trials. To turn Queen's Evidence, he had to now formally admit his guilt to the court regarding the armed robbery. Which he did. I next had to obtain a lengthy written statement from him, fully admitting the preparation and involvement of both in the armed robbery. I took this statement in the cell area below the court. It took almost two hours. The court became very irritated with me for taking so long and kept trying to rush me. But I would not be rushed, as this was a vital piece of court evidence and had to be done properly.

The trial at the Old Bailey took several days. It was quite gruelling, as I was the only Flying Squad detective there. Our prosecuting barrister, a woman, was competent in her own way, but I had to help her by passing her prompts I had written on pieces of paper during her cross-examination of the defendants. She used these prompts as questions in court. For instance, one of the defendants said he had caught a bus to the street where he was arrested just to do some shopping and said he had nothing to do with the attempted robbery. One of my hand-written notes passed to our barrister told her that no bus tickets or cash were found in his pockets when he was arrested. Jokingly and outside of court, the two defending barristers suggested that I was a covert prosecutor by handing her notes! Anyway, I sportingly allowed her to buy me a few beers and a meal upon the day of their conviction. Throughout my many professional appearances at court, I discovered that barristers were a superior breed to solicitors.

The jury found the former security van driver guilty of the armed robbery. Both received a sentence of fourteen years in prison. However, there was a strange twist to all this. Several months later, one of the detectives who had arrested the armed robbers was investigated by the police complaints unit for malpractice with his drug offence investigations. Although the complaints were not connected with his arrest of the armed robbers, it tainted any evidence that he had given by calling into question his honesty and integrity. As a result, the armed robber who had been a security van driver was released from prison. As you may remember, he told the court that he was not guilty and that it was a case of mistaken identity. Unfairly perhaps, the armed robber who had turned Queen's Evidence against the former security van driver was not released as he had previously admitted his guilt to the court.

I was involved in the arrest of a gang of armed robbers who had decided to do 'one last job'.

They were well past the retirement age for 'armed blaggers'. As I was taking the fingerprints of one of them, he asked me what the going rate for getting bail was. I told him that he may have been able to bribe his way out on bail in years gone by, but those days had passed. He shrugged and seemed to accept my response.

I noticed that Rigg's corridor walls were lined with photos of wanted armed robbers taken from bank and building society security cameras. No real use was made of this vital evidence. I used to show these photos to my informant. He recognised a few, and this resulted in arrests and convictions. The value of video evidence was therefore brought home to me. I was to use this experience later in my career to rather excellent effect.

The new detective chief inspector wanted to replace a detective sergeant at Rigg. Indeed, he asked me if I knew of a suitable detective sergeant who wished to work there. A few weeks later, a detective sergeant was posted to Rigg. He had worked with the DCI in the past. Unknown to me at that time, he was to be my replacement.

An armed robber regularly committed robberies against betting shops in East London. He drove a red Ford Escort. Nothing more was known. I was on my way to an enquiry with another detective when I saw a red Ford Escort pull up outside a betting shop in Wood Green, northeast London. The driver went into the betting shop. The detective and I both looked at each other and, without a word being said, we decided to investigate. Neither of us was armed. Inside the betting shop, our man was gazing at the racing form on the wall. We split up and did the same. My plan was that, once he had done the robbery and his guard was slightly down, we would rush him and seize the gun. What could possibly go wrong? After a few minutes, he placed a bet and left. I can't say I was disappointed; I was also somewhat relieved. We did not mention this to anyone and just took it as part of the job. I discovered that armed robbers, when in prison, were regarded by other prisoners as being the elite. One burglar told me they were respected for risking their lives as they faced being ambushed and shot by the Flying Squad.

The Flying Squad at Rigg was now notorious for having fights between themselves in restaurants. It was almost a macho expectation. As a result, many venues banned them. There was a function at a restaurant in the Seven Sisters area of North London that I attended. It was either Greek or Turkish. The meal started in the late afternoon, and we were the only diners present. The tables were in rows. I had been at

Rigg for about six months by now, and I felt that I was perhaps beginning to be accepted, despite the new DCI's presence. The wine and beer flowed, and I was almost beginning to enjoy myself.

One of our detective sergeants joined us late as he had been committed elsewhere. To catch up with our drinking, he started drinking wine in half-pint glasses. He was well known for drinking wine in half-pint glasses. Later, I went to the toilet. Blocking me at the door was this same detective sergeant. Growling at me, he asked what my team of detectives had achieved recently and suggested that it was "probably fuck all". As a witty response, I said that even if it was "probably fuck all", it would still be more than his team achieved. I thought that this response was quite witty and something that Oscar Wilde would have been proud of. His response was to head-butt me. The blow was hard, and I felt as though I was one of those Tom and Jerry cartoon characters, whose body transformed into multiple cracks when hit with an anvil. I asked him why he had done this, but he just growled. I then started to walk away, but I felt angry at this unjustified assault. I turned and confronted him. A struggle started, and we rolled across tables and onto the floor. Others broke up the struggle. The DCI was present and found it all amusing; his attitude condoned such behaviour and perhaps actively encouraged it. I had been dragged down to his level. How pointless it all was.

The next day, the detective sergeant who had head-butted me gave me a bottle of scotch. He put it on my desk and walked away without saying a word. I could have had him arrested for assaulting me, but what would have been the point? Despite having a violent nature, he was a very competent detective. He obviously saw me as a threat for some reason or other.

I now felt as though I was in some sort of bizarre Wild West scenario, where the new rules were decided by the DCI and his 'inner sanctum'.

To my surprise, I was asked to play rugby for Rigg Approach at a tournament against the other three Flying Squad departments. I hadn't played rugby for about ten years, but I agreed to play. I was quite fit then. On the day of the tournament, I discovered that only four players from Rigg Approach turned up. The other eleven who I thought would be playing did not appear in the changing room. In their places were players from established clubs such as Saracens and Wasps, who had no connection with the police. The game was fast, and I almost scored a try. I was asked to play in a subsequent game but declined. Had I been singled out? And if so, why?

A symbolic event occurred in September 1992, about eleven months after I first arrived at Rigg. I was in 'The Ship Aground' pub near to Rigg having a drink. With me at the bar were the DCI and a detective sergeant from Rigg. The DCI turned to me and said that if he had been involved in my selection, I would never have been accepted. He said that what I had done at West Ham in securing the conviction of a corrupt detective sergeant was totally unacceptable to him. He told me to resign from the Flying Squad as soon as possible. One of the gunship drivers collected the three of us and took us to Rigg.

The next day, I was asked to attend the DCI's office. With him was a detective inspector. The DCI told me that I didn't 'gel' with him and that he could not 'trust' me. He told me to leave the Flying Squad as soon as possible. It was obviously not an issue of my professional performance but something else. I suggested that, even if I arrested a team of bank robbers every week, he would still feel the same. He agreed. He then stated that if I did not leave voluntarily, he would write a very damning annual appraisal of me which was due the next month. If I left voluntarily, he said that my appraisal would be average. To play for time, I told him that I would have to think about this offer, and he agreed. I then left his office and considered my options.

I was studying for the inspector's promotion exam back then. As the date of the examination was approaching, I took two weeks' leave to study. Upon my return to Rigg, my security swipe card at the entrance door would not work. Having rung the bell, I was admitted to the building. The DCI then phoned and told me that I was not to enter as I 'could not be trusted'. He stated that I had a direct line to the 'complaints branch'. Also, I was not to enter the building unless I was under supervision throughout my time there. He admitted that he had deactivated my door entry swipe card. This was both unfair and humiliating. Someone must have contacted the DCI to say that I was in the building for him to ring me. I could not understand why having an honest detective on the Flying Squad was considered such an impediment by the DCI and DI.

About a week later, I had a request to see the DCI in his office. Sat with him was the same DI. The DCI asked me if I was going to resign from my post. I replied no as I had done nothing wrong. He then handed me the appraisal report they had both signed. I sat and read it. It was a farce of a report. Most of the appraisal categories showed me as performing almost as bad as theoretically possible. Instead of using a surgical scalpel against me, the DCI had used a blunt axe. His comments were ludicrous to the point of hilarity. I asked him if I could take a photocopy, and he agreed. (I still have that copy).

Within a couple of days, I received a phone call from a very senior police officer at New Scotland Yard. He told me to leave Rigg immediately for my own safety and that I was now posted as an attachment from that day onwards to the Anti-Terrorist Branch at New Scotland Yard. I was told not to collect my personal items from Rigg or empty my desk. As an attachment, my position was not permanent but only temporary. (However, I was interviewed six months later for the permanent position of detective sergeant and was successful).

Shortly after joining the Anti-Terrorist Branch, I submitted an official report to the Flying Squad senior management at New Scotland Yard expressing all my concerns. I pointed out that a recent commissioner's commendation regarding an attempted murder had not been mentioned within the fake appraisal. Also, no mention had been made of my successful underworld informant or the fact that he had been awarded £4,000 at New Scotland Yard by the deputy commissioner for his information. I also added that I had been denied vital training courses. Additionally, there had been no prior written warnings regarding my alleged atrocious performance for the previous year. This appraisal was the opposite of all appraisals during my police service, both before Rigg Approach and subsequently.

It was agreed by Flying Squad senior management at New Scotland Yard that I had been unfairly treated. The DCI and his DI were given 'words of advice'. This is police jargon to say that they were advised by more senior officers that their conduct towards me had been wrong. I was not satisfied with this result. Shortly afterwards, at New Scotland Yard, the head of the Flying Squad requested to see me. On entering his office, he did not invite me to be seated. His demeanour was hostile. Without looking up at me from his desk, he asked if there was anything else I wanted. I replied that I could not understand why the DCI and DI who had concocted my appraisal were still in post at Rigg Approach. He did not answer. He then dismissed me from his office. I was treated as if I was nothing but an irritating pest.

Several years later, while they were still serving at Rigg, the following detectives were officially dealt with for corruption. The DCI was suspected of corruption, and his home was searched by anti-corruption police officers. The detective sergeant who replaced me was convicted of corruption and served a prison sentence. The DI who, along with the DCI, had concocted a false appraisal for me was convicted of corruption and served a prison sentence. Three other detective constables and a detective sergeant also serving at Rigg were convicted of corruption and served prison sentences. All these detectives were convicted of their corrupt activities at Rigg. There is a Russian saying: a fish rots at the head first.

Following these arrests, all detectives at Rigg were then treated by the Crown Prosecution Service as being unreliable witnesses for court. I was the only exception to this rule.

I would like to stress that most detectives at Rigg Approach were not corrupt. Hard to say how many exactly, but I would estimate that at least 70% were not corrupt. However, those who were corrupt included supervisors. These corrupt detectives were known as the 'inner sanctum', and ensured that the others, including me, were excluded from their corrupt activities.

On occasion, I worked with detectives from the Flying Squad based at Finchley; they were different compared to Rigg Approach. They were far more professional. I think the management there had a far more positive influence. With that wonderful gift of hindsight, I would have preferred to have been based at Finchley.

In 1997, the Met's complaints unit mounted a 'sting' operation. Three detectives from Rigg Approach were arrested. The 'sting' comprised an unoccupied flat in East London where officers from the complaints team secretly placed a large quantity of cannabis. The three detectives were discreetly made aware of the cannabis. On covert video, all three detectives were recorded entering the flat and stealing the cannabis. Two were convicted and sentenced to a term in prison. While there, both became 'super-grasses' and provided information about other detectives at Rigg Approach. The third detective told the jury at the Old Bailey that he thought he was part of the recovery of a 'civil debt' and knew nothing about the drugs. The jury believed him, and he was released.

Martin Heslop QC, defending a detective constable said: "There existed within the Rigg Approach division of the Flying Squad what can only be described as a culture of corruption involving secrecy, camaraderie, and dishonesty between the officers. The corruption was well established and extended from top to bottom and reflected a code of conduct based on team membership and loyalty to that team. You either fell in, or your career in it ended abruptly".

In my view, there had been a breakdown in discipline within Rigg Approach. This has occurred in military units and resulted in the unit being disbanded in disgrace. Perhaps Rigg Approach should have been disbanded after it was recognised that the management had treated me appallingly? The signs were there and should have been acted upon.

The Flying Squad is different today. It no longer has a rogue element and is totally professional. The building at Rigg was disposed of, and today's Flying Squad detectives now work from Barking Police Station.

Detective Sergeant Anti-Terrorist Branch New Scotland Yard 1992–1998

I cannot describe in full detail all the activities I was involved in during my time with the Anti-Terrorist Branch. I cannot specify exactly the dates and locations of events, and I cannot reveal techniques and tactics. To do so may compromise future operations. I hope the reader understands this restriction. I will, however, do my best to ensure that the demands and risks met by all counter-terrorist agencies are accurately impressed upon the reader.

I can make clear, however, as to what a joy and relief it was to leave the Flying Squad at Rigg Approach. I had left the oppressive and hostile atmosphere behind and now had the opportunity to start afresh. The Anti-Terrorist Branch was completely different to Rigg. It was professional, and the detectives were of a higher calibre in general than those at Rigg. The senior management was also vastly superior. There were a few former Flying Squad detectives in senior posts, but they were nothing like the management I had to deal with at Rigg. None had ever served there. The detective chief superintendent on the Anti-Terrorist Branch was a former Flying Squad detective and had served at Finchley Flying Squad. His rank now was equivalent to that of an assistant chief constable. He was one of the best detectives I have ever worked with.

The top rank of the Anti-Terrorist Branch was that of a commander. Next ranks were a detective chief superintendent, two detective superintendents and three detective chief inspectors. The rest comprised six detective inspectors, detective sergeants, and detective constables. A small number of uniform officers also worked in plain clothes.

There were six small teams of detectives available for investigative tasks and arrests. These comprised detective constables and detective sergeants. On a good day, there would be a total of about twenty of these detectives on duty to provide national coverage. There was also a team of detectives who specialised in the processing of exhibits recovered during terrorist investigations. A few detectives were firearms and surveillance trained. Additionally, we had two highly experienced civilian members to provide national and international advice regarding explosive devices. We also had expert civilian computer analysts to assist with complex investigations, as well as officers who staffed the HOLMES (Home Office Major Enquiry System) computers, which were an essential aid both to investigations and prosecutions.

We had a responsibility to investigate all terrorist incidents in England and Wales. (Since the terrorist attacks of 9/11, the Anti-Terrorist Branch has greatly expanded and has been known as the counter-terrorist command since 2006. Also in 2006, the Metropolitan Police Special Branch merged with the counter-terrorist command).

There was a control room, which provided an immediate coordinated response to terrorist activity in London and was manned 24/7 by a detective sergeant and three detective constables. All calls from members of the public and other police forces were routed through here for assessment and action. A vital role of the control room was the response to bomb warnings from the IRA. We were plagued with bomb hoaxes from the public and could not respond to the dozens of hoaxes that took place daily. Civilian casualties (particularly children) were seen by the IRA as detrimental to their propaganda cause, and they tried to avoid this from happening. The warnings were usually one hour, which was little time to deploy resources and protect the public. It became very demanding for us when the IRA placed bombs in different locations within London at the same time.

An IRA bomb warning would state a location and the time the bomb was due to go off. Upon receiving this message, we would deploy specialists to the location given. The location of the bomb would be taped off by uniform officers from the local police, and the public evacuated.

Responsibility for bombs outside of London fell to army bomb disposal teams.

The detective sergeant supervising the control room also held the keys to the armoury and was responsible for the issue and return of firearms and ammunition.

Special Branch occupied the floor above us at New Scotland Yard. It manned security desks at airports and ports and was responsible for national security. Special Branch officers had received detective training at Hendon but had not served in CID offices. Their numbers were many times more than us. They had little experience in criminal investigation. Special

Branch generally recruited police officers when they only had two years of police experience and had just finished their probationary period. We at the Anti-Terrorist Branch were all very experienced detectives, and our principal role was the investigation of terrorist offences and presenting these cases at the Old Bailey. Another role of Special Branch was direct liaison with MI5 (security services).

Shortly after I joined, there was a profound development: MI5 officially announced their existence to the world. MI5 also now took the lead regarding terrorist matters.

One of my first assignments was the arrest of a suspected IRA bomber in West London. I and three other detectives went to the suspect's address to carry out the arrest. We were not armed, and we did not wear body armour, as was the norm at that time. We had no information to suggest that he was armed, and we acted accordingly. (Today, no such chances would be taken). He was arrested under the terrorism act, and his residence was searched. In many ways, this was no different from usual police procedures. We had no extra powers compared to other detectives, and the investigation followed standard procedures. We were not politically motivated; it was just a job to us. Prior to being on the Anti-Terrorist Branch, all detectives would have served for some years investigating offences such as murder, rape, and burglary. Having then served for four or five years, investigating terrorist offences, these detectives would be returned to their usual duties as Met CID detectives.

One of the significant differences between the Anti-Terrorist Branch and my previous roles were the vast investigative resources available to us; if we needed anything, it was just a phone call away. There was no waiting for equipment requests – they arrived that day! Also, we had the full support of the public. Even criminals would help by providing us with information. Our morale was high, and I felt that, at last, I was appreciated and valued for my work.

Just after being assigned to the Anti-Terrorist Branch, I was informed that I had passed the written section of the inspector's exam. My studies for the exam had taken place while I was at Rigg. Despite all the pressures and distractions, I was successful. I treated my new colleagues to a few beers in celebration. This success did not mean immediate promotion: there were three more stages yet to complete over the next five years. The delay of five years was brought about by a report into the conditions of police service instigated by then-Prime Minister John Major. This report resulted in the national loss of certain allowances and the removal of the rank of chief inspector from the promotion process. The report was, of course, all about saving the government money. The knock-on effect was that all promotion in the police came to a halt for five years until another government report recommended reinstating the rank of chief inspector.

Another notable aspect of my work was that, due to of my role, I was expected to advise chief constables as to what course of action they should take regarding imminent terrorist matters. Role, not rank, was the order of the day. Our training, experience, and abilities were essential in our role as anti-terrorist detectives.

On many occasions, I provided lectures on terrorist matters nationally to such groups as MI5, the National Police College, the military, and other agencies. I enjoyed giving these presentations, and I think I had a flair for it. I received numerous written compliments for my presentation skills. I was, at one time, assigned for a week to a specialist army unit to provide five presentations per day for a week. It was quite a challenge, but I enjoyed it. I had felt isolated, ignored, and despised during my time at Rigg. Now, I was beginning to bloom.

Something significant struck me during this time: CCTV was now everywhere and had become a cornerstone of police investigations. I established that the Anti-Terrorist Branch had limited capacity for processing this vital evidence. In my view, high-quality video evidence that clearly identifies the criminal is better than DNA and fingerprint evidence. Video evidence could tell the jury what the criminal was doing, what he was wearing, who he was with, and how long he was there for. It could also prove if the accused was innocent. In other words, video evidence was a silent and impartial witness. DNA and fingerprint evidence can only say that the criminal was present at the crime scene at some time in the past.

I then embarked upon a national crusade to improve not only the quality of CCTV evidence but also to improve police processes regarding CCTV evidence. In hand with this herculean task, I sought to improve the quality of covert video evidence provided by the police regarding their own undercover investigations. In a short time, I took the lead nationally. To cut a long story short, the IRA referred to me as 'the Video King'.

I spent much of my time at the Met video laboratory processing masses of video evidence. The laboratory was manned by highly competent and dedicated individuals who worked under constant pressure. They saw the worst sides of human behaviour and included the processing of evidence against paedophiles. Their working life was in almost permanent semi-darkness, only punctuated by intermittent flashing lights and the occasional cup of tea. I was able to secure them significant government funding to purchase the latest equipment in our ongoing struggle against terrorism.

Unfortunately, the senior management of the technical unit at New Scotland Yard did not welcome my crusade to improve the quality of CCTV evidence. My crusade not only related to public CCTV systems but also to police cameras installed by the Met's technical unit. I wanted to ensure the recordings were good enough to confirm that the person seen in the video was the same as the person standing in the dock at court. The standard for all criminal trials was that the prosecution must prove their case beyond all reasonable doubt. This was the standard for video clarity that I sought. The boss of the technical unit viewed me as the biggest challenge of his career. He was quite open about it. I think he resented that a detective should impinge upon his profession.

I had no technical training, but I knew what was needed for court purposes. Too often, the recordings the technical unit made were too poor in quality to be of value in court. Normally, the police would accept this and not complain. I wanted the tail to stop wagging the dog. We police officers had a duty to obtain the best evidence, particularly for terrorist investigations. I would be asked technical questions by his staff, as if to catch me out. I would reply that I did not know the answer, but that was not the point: it was up to them to provide images of an evidential standard, not me. There was also some concern from the police side that I was stepping beyond my boundaries as a detective.

What was my view of the IRA? I had been involved in numerous arrests, and I have to say that there was no 'typical profile' of an IRA member – they were all from various backgrounds and ages. They were, of course, highly motivated, and as far as I could tell, were paid little for the risks they took. In my experience, all were male. In general terms, I found them to be intelligent but, in my opinion, misguided. I had no personal animosity towards them; I was simply part of the judicial process. It was said that, upon arrest, they expected to be tortured. This did not happen and was quite a surprise to them. I always made a point of providing tea after. We did not expect confessions, and we built our court case around forensic evidence. Any interview was a waste of time, in my opinion, as the response was always "no comment" upon their solicitor's advice. But we had to persevere with our questions, as it was their entitlement to hear the extent of our case.

Four members of an IRA unit who had been under surveillance were arrested at gunpoint on a railway platform in London. They were ordered to lie face down and were handcuffed. However, a fifth man was lying face down and handcuffed. I knelt and spoke to him. He said, "Honest, I've paid my fare. My ticket's in my back pocket. Bit over the top for fare evasion, isn't it?" He was a member of the public who had innocently found himself caught up in all this. I soon established that we had no interest in him. I released him and thanked him for his patience, and he was delighted to catch the next train for home.

We were also involved in investigations regarding Loyalist Paramilitary offences, but this was not on the same scale as IRA investigations. It should be noted that Northern Ireland police investigated terrorist offences within their jurisdiction, and we in the Anti-Terrorist Branch were not directly involved. However, there were occasions when I was required to fly to Northern Ireland to investigate IRA offences in England.

The first time I went to Northern Ireland was

not in an anti-terrorist role, however. I was working with Scotland Yard's extradition unit, and our job was to bring back an IRA member who was wanted in the USA to face arms charges. I did feel slightly apprehensive, but having met our RUC contacts, I realised that this was not a particularly dangerous operation for them. We stayed overnight at a hotel some miles away from Belfast. One of the Royal Ulster Constabulary (RUC) detectives was female. She placed her handbag down on the hotel bar, and it made a heavy metallic thud. I did not have to guess what was in the handbag.

In the morning, we collected the IRA member from custody in Belfast and took him to Belfast airport to fly him back to London. All the airlines refused to take him on board as they viewed him as a security risk. We had no option but to fly him back in an RAF Islander aircraft. The Islander was a small twin-engine aircraft driven by propellers. It had no cabin pressurisation. In my opinion, it was an upgraded Wellington bomber of WW2 vintage. The RAF charged the Anti-Terrorist Branch £10,000 for their assistance.

I had further assignments to Northern Ireland and found the countryside outstandingly beautiful. I began to realise that terrorism only related to a tiny proportion of the population;

the vast majority just wanted to be left in peace to get on with their lives. Many of my RUC hosts were not concerned should there be a united Ireland. Some had married Catholics, and a significant number of officers within the RUC were also Catholic. The situation was certainly not as portrayed by the media, who only concentrated on the divisions and violence.

The RUC did not have a specialist unit investigating terrorism. This was surprising to me. Local detectives investigated explosions and shootings. The main difference I noticed between Scotland Yard detectives and the RUC was that RUC detectives were always armed with a handgun for their own protection. The striking similarity was that we all enjoyed an off-duty beer or two.

Little of my activity in Northern Ireland related to Belfast. It is not widely understood that the heart of the IRA lay in the border areas between Southern and Northern Ireland. Areas such as South Armagh were impossible to police in the conventional sense due to their strong IRA presence. The RUC had heavily fortified police stations such as Bessbrook, and any police activity was often only performed with an army escort. One of my RUC hosts in Belfast told me that he had never been to the border areas and had no wish to do so; he said life in Belfast was far safer!

As a result of a terrorist investigation into offences on the mainland, I and a colleague visited a house in South Armagh. Armed, plain-clothed RUC officers escorted us in two plain cars from a nearby fortified police station. Ideally, the army should have escorted us, but they were committed elsewhere on that day. We spoke to the occupants of the house for some minutes. As we drove away, we came under attack from all sides by a mob throwing bricks and other objects. This caused us some concern as the IRA could have prepared an ambush for us on the only road leaving the area. There was the possibility of one of the IRA active service units lying in wait for us with a heavy machine gun. There was no further attack against us, and we went to the next address nearby as part of our investigation. From here, we drove back to the RUC police station, where we all enjoyed a rather 'strong' cup of tea or two!

At about this time, I visited Newry on the Irish border. The police station at Newry was also an army base for the area. The Parachute Regiment had suffered heavy losses back in 1979 close to Newry at Warrenpoint, when their trucks were blown up as they drove past a hidden bomb. The IRA bomb was detonated by wire from within the nearby Irish border. A second hidden bomb was detonated as rescue attempts were being made. Eighteen soldiers were killed. My visit to Newry was to interview the manager of a commercial premise in connection with IRA offences on the mainland. While at the police station, we were all warned of a possible IRA mortar attack from a nearby vehicle. There was no attack, but they were apprehensive moments for us all. There is no hiding from mortar bombs as they drop vertically from the sky. Back in 1985, nine members of the RUC were killed when an IRA mortar bomb exploded within Newry Police Station. Seven of the dead officers were Protestant; two were Catholic.

I walked from Newry Police Station to my destination. It was a five-minute walk. What was slightly eerie was that I was escorted by soldiers and RUC police officers. Each junction ahead was covered with rifles by my escorts as I progressed. I think I represented the long arm of the law that stretched from New Scotland Yard. I was dressed in a suit and tie; I was the only one in our group not wearing body armour, and I had a briefcase rather than a gun. Is the pen mightier than the sword? My task complete, we returned to Newry Police Station.

Back at New Scotland Yard, I was asked to carry out a slightly unusual task. A member of an IRA terrorist cell in London had been under surveillance. By chance, a uniform police car happened to stop the car he was driving. The officer requested to see the driver's documents. The driver did not have them with him. The officer therefore requested him to produce his driving documents at a police station within the next seven days and issued him with the appropriate form. The IRA member did not attend a police station to have his driving documents checked. This presented a problem: if the IRA member did not have an official visit from the authorities regarding his failure to comply within seven days, he could well have suspected that his cover had been blown. I was given the task to visit him at his residence and pretend that I was simply an administrator carrying out a routine clerical task regarding his failure to produce his driving documents.

I parked my car nearby and walked to his residence. I had with me a large clipboard, which is the badge of an administrator the world over. Officers were parked nearby in a backup vehicle. The front door opened. I explained who I was, and I politely asked to see his driving documents. He invited me inside. This gave me a chance to make a mental note of the layout and contents of the flat for any future police raid. There was no one else present. His driving documents appeared to be in order. I thanked him and left the residence. I'm sure that he did not suspect my real intentions. It seemed a long walk back to my car.

One of my responsibilities was to be the liaison point with MI5 surveillance teams. As part of that function, I was invited for a meal with my contact at the Special Forces Club in Knightsbridge. The club motto was 'Spirit of Resistance' and was then a private members club. The club was on several floors and had rooms for an overnight stay. It was formed in 1945 in honour of those secret agents who had died at the hands of the Nazis in WW2. We had a drink at the bar, and I noticed some women of a certain age were seated and having drinks. They had names such as Vera and Violet. These women in WW2, I was told, had been secret agents in France, spying on the Germans and organising sabotage. The walls and corridors were adorned with photographs of secret agents from the past. The meal was superb and the service excellent. The decor and atmosphere were from a time long gone. It had been a privilege to be invited by my host.

As I mentioned previously from my Flying Squad days, informants are vital for police investigations. They are hard to find and retain. During one of my enquiries with the Anti-Terrorist Branch, I was able to find an informant regarding terrorism. Such informants are extremely difficult to acquire. He was not an informant with access to the highest grade of intelligence, but he was proving useful to us. I had concerns that his personal safety had been compromised and immediately found him a 'safe house'. To do this, I had to be given a false identity and false documents, which included a credit card and driving licence in a false name. In a short time, I had to memorise all these details and practice the signature on my card. It was important I could convince anyone if challenged as to my new identity. To have failed would possibly have not only put the informant's life at risk but also jeopardised future police operations. I was successful. My success not only protected his identity and safety as an informant, but it also ensured that we continued to have a reliable source of terrorist information.

By now, I had come to realise that I was respected and appreciated by MI5, SO13, and Special Branch. At Rigg Approach on the Flying Squad, I had been despised by the management and their associates. I had been heading for a loss of my career or possibly worse. Now, I was back in the saddle and ready for anything that might come my way. My working days had become long and unpredictable. The risks were unknown, but I would not have had it any other way. I was now in my element. Ironically, Rigg had unintentionally introduced me to the best move of my career: the Anti-Terrorist Branch. Perhaps that terrible year had been worthwhile after all.

One of the most interesting aspects of my time with the Anti-Terrorist Branch was working in Ireland – or Eire, as it is more correctly known. In many ways, this was a world away from Northern Ireland. Obviously, Ireland is not in the United Kingdom and is a sovereign state. There were detectives on SO13 who would not go to Ireland as they thought it was unsafe and they might be assassinated by the IRA. After all, Ireland was often seen as a safe base for the IRA. I did not share their view, although I could understand their fears. My assessment of the IRA was that their cause was for a united Ireland. To date, they had not targeted members of the mainland police such as me. They were, of course, responsible for the murders of many, many RUC officers.

I found Ireland to be as beautiful as Northern Ireland. They shared the same shades of deep green pastures, hedges, and trees. Indeed, the boundary between the two was artificial but agreed upon by both countries in 1922, following the Irish War of Independence. I do not wish to become involved in the politics of the island of Ireland here – it is complex and was, at times, unfathomable to me. For instance, there is an Orange Order of Protestants in Ireland.

Without going into detail, my new task with a colleague was of a sensitive political nature. It could have had a detrimental impact upon the Good Friday Agreement of 1998 had we failed. Much of our work centred on the Dublin area. We would fly from London City Airport under false names and addresses to be met by our host detectives from the *Garda Siochana* (Irish police) at Dublin airport. We were treated with absolute courtesy and friendliness by our hosts. We stayed at excellent hotels in Dublin and were accompanied every evening by *Garda* detectives for a Guinness or two. However, we had serious work ahead of us.

The Garda detectives were helpful in our enquiries. I asked one of them if he was at risk being seen to help us. His response was unexpected. He said that he had a few big brothers and had nothing to fear from the IRA. To him, the IRA was not composed of supermen. Many in the Garda had attended the same schools as IRA members. They knew who the IRA men were but did not necessarily know what they were up to in Britain. There was a suggestion in the past that the Garda were ambivalent regarding the IRA and saw them as a problem for Northern Ireland and not themselves. However, the IRA shot dead a Garda detective during a raid on a security cash van. This did not go down well with the Garda, and attitudes hardened.

After our sixth visit to Dublin, there was a sudden change of circumstances: we were now provided with protection by an armed Garda detective assigned to each of us. Wherever we went, an armed guard was with us. I asked why there had been this change, and the officer could not supply me with an answer. He said that he was just doing his job as directed. Obviously, there had been intelligence received that our lives were at risk from the IRA. Had the IRA attacked us, I don't think that these two Garda detectives could, even with the best intentions at heart, have saved us – handguns against automatic rifles were not an even match. I respect the Garda detectives to this day for being willing to take this risk to protect our lives.

On one of my visits to Dublin, I was queuing for the Dublin flight at Stansted airport along with about one hundred other passengers. I was dressed casually along with everyone else, and two men approached me from airport security, asking me to accompany them. I was led away to a small cubicle, and they asked to search my briefcase. These men were from Special Branch. They opened my case, and I said nothing. In it were various Anti-Terrorist Branch documents. I showed them my identification. I then received a flight upgrade.

As in Northern Ireland, I came to realise that the vast majority in the country just wanted to get on with their lives and had absolutely no interest in violence.

Eventually, my visits to Dublin came to an end. The Good Friday Agreement brought a cessation of terrorism in Northern Ireland.

Towards the end of my time with the Anti-Terrorist Branch, I had been granted the rank of acting detective inspector. This permitted me to supervise armed surveillance operations. These operations were composed of an armed surveillance team, armed police officers, and an arrest team. These operations could last for many days and extend across the country. We were always short of sleep, but the adrenalin kept us going. I was highly accountable for my decisions, which were monitored at a government level. There was a control room at Scotland Yard that provided support, but ultimately, the decisions were mine. It was a responsibility that I thrived upon.

One Saturday morning, I parked my car in a

parking zone in North London that was free to park during the weekend. I was due to work no more than eight hours supervising the control room staff. However, a terrorist incident occurred in London, and I was not able to return to my car until Monday evening. I found a parking ticket attached to my windscreen. A senior officer contacted the local authority for parking enforcement, explained the circumstances, and asked that the fine be waived. The local authority (Haringey Borough) refused the waiver.

I mentioned earlier how the courts could be disdainful and aggressive towards police officers. Here is another example that occurred while I was on the Anti-Terrorist Branch. At the Old Bailey, I had been involved in presenting complex video evidence to the court for several days. On one occasion after the court had finished for the day, I spent time using court equipment situated in a separate room for the benefit of the CPS.

The next day, the court clerk ripped into me in anger. His tone was extremely aggressive and insulting. The court clerk is not a judge but assists the judge in their deliberations. He wears a barrister-style wig. Apparently, I had left one or two wires disconnected among the video equipment. I became angry and let fly with both barrels. I told him that he would never have spoken to a defence lawyer in these terms. I also told him that he would never have spoken in this way to a defendant or witness, that he should treat police officers with respect. He was absolutely stunned by my response. Good. One of the court ushers came up to me later and told me that she had enjoyed my response, as he had deserved it. So, there I was, in conflict with both terrorists and court staff.

Within my last few months with the Anti-Terrorist Branch, a detective superintendent supervised the creation of a terrorist-related crime prevention poster that would be distributed throughout the country. The poster had taken some time to create and be approved. Thousands were printed and stored in bags within the basement of New Scotland Yard, ready for distribution. At this point, the plan went very wrong. The bags they were stored in were similar looking to waste bags. One day, operatives collected all these bags, thinking they were waste. They were all transported to the Met police incinerator in South London and disposed of; no more posters were produced. The detective superintendent was philosophical and took it better than I expected. He had been a career Special Branch detective and told me that his recent transfer to the Anti-Terrorist Branch concerned him at first. He thought that he might not be accepted as we were viewed as quite a hardened bunch of detectives who did not suffer fools gladly. He turned out not to be a fool, and he earned my respect and that of many others.

Additionally, I had now been awarded a Bachelor of Science degree with Honours in Police Studies. The Met had sponsored me for this qualification. I had studied in what spare time I had on the Anti-Terrorist Branch, and very often at the last minute – such was the nature of the fight against terrorism. Has this qualification been of any use to me? Probably not, but I did learn something about the complexities of statistics.

By now, I had passed the final selection process for the rank of detective inspector. I had held the rank of acting detective inspector on the Anti-Terrorist Branch for the previous year. I could have stayed on the Anti-Terrorist Branch as a detective inspector as a CCTV/video specialist, but I decided that a career change was best. The previous years had been very demanding, and in my view at the time, a change was as good as a rest.

My transfer to a police station was made complicated by recent events at Rigg Approach, my former Flying Squad posting. The corruption convictions of detectives at Rigg Approach had caused my posting to a police station in the East

London area to be untenable. The tentacles of corruption extended beyond Rigg Approach; certain detectives in East London had not been arrested but were involved in serious corruption and had links with Rigg. Some of these detectives outranked me and could have destroyed my career or caused me harm. I rejected postings offered in East London and opted for a posting in Haringey, North London. This process delayed my promotion by almost a year.

Detective Inspector Haringey Borough 1998–2005

With now almost eighteen years' police service, I again found myself posted to Haringey but this time as a detective inspector.

What does a detective inspector do? There are many definitions. I saw myself as someone who used his authority to terminate malicious or pointless crime investigations. Such investigations drained resources that could be used on more important and relevant investigations. The CID could not investigate every serious crime reported, particularly within London boroughs such as Haringey. They did not have the resources to cope. In practice, it meant that, at the start and end of every day, I would review all reported serious crimes and ensure that only the most viable were investigated.

Many crimes are reported with a hidden

agenda. For instance, I have never known a genuine offence of 'aggravated burglary'. In essence, aggravated burglary means a house has been broken into and the occupants threatened or attacked while their valuables and cash were stolen. This is a serious offence, with a maximum penalty of over twenty years in prison. However, in my experience, I found that every aggravated burglary reported was in fact a result of a drugs war, where one side broke in to steal money and drugs from the other side. The facts were, of course, very, very elusive. Unfortunately, senior uniform officers often took such crimes at face value and demanded CID officers be delegated to investigate as a matter of urgency. I refused to play the 'headless-chicken' game and run around in circles. This, of course, put me at odds with senior management. It also did not help that I was always right in the end.

The military granted detective inspectors and ranks above commissioned officer status when resident at a military base. This allowed them access to the officer's mess. As a perhaps interesting point, when I was an officer in the Royal Navy, I outranked the Met commissioner during ceremonial occasions.

In many ways, I was a sieve that prevented cases of low evidential worth clogging up the Crown Prosecution Service and the rest of the judicial system. This did not always make me popular with our uniform colleagues, who became angry when we occasionally had no choice but to release suspects due to insufficient evidence. This was through no fault of the uniform officers or the investigating detectives.

Another of my roles was to ensure that detectives worked hard. A good source of information to identify the lazy detective constable was to listen to their supervising detective sergeants. These detective sergeants were able to identify those who were causing problems. It was always in the detective constables' interests that the lazy ones were removed from post and replaced by hard workers to equally share the incessant investigative workload. My previous experience as a detective constable taught me how demoralising it was to have a fellow detective constable shirking his responsibilities. It was especially demoralising if the detective inspector failed to confront such poor performance. Too many detective inspectors preferred an easy life without any staff confrontation.

I also saw my role as a defender of CID staff against unjust criticism. Unjust criticism, often of a malicious form, would sometimes be made by members of the public. Ironically, the most frequent unjust comments were made by senior uniform management with no CID experience. Often, they had made a superficial and cursory assessment of an investigation and decided to criticise the detective constable directly and without consultation first with myself or a detective sergeant.

The CID office in practice was run by detective sergeants. They were equivalent to non- commissioned officers (NCOs) in the military, such as sergeants and corporals. My time in the Royal Navy convinced me that NCOs were the backbone of the military services.

The role of a detective inspector in the public's mind has been confused by fictionalised television detective inspectors. As a detective inspector, I did not break down doors at dawn or chase fleeing criminals; this was the role of detective constables and detective sergeants. To have joined them in such tasks would have undermined the authority of the detective sergeants. Additionally, they all would have wondered if they were under increased supervision due to poor performance.

The reality of my role was management, and it was largely desk-bound. It was not a role that I enjoyed, but having made my bed, I had to lie on it. The worst aspect of my role was the non-stop management meetings I had to attend. Each one lasted at least an hour and should either never have been called or lasted at most for twenty minutes – if I chaired a meeting, it would be over within twenty minutes. Many meetings were chaired by senior officers who loved the sound of their own voice and could bore for England and Europe as they droned on and on, spewing out management cliché upon management cliché. Many managers enjoyed meetings as there was no requirement for responsibility or immediate decision-making.

I decided to apply for promotion to the rank of detective chief inspector. However, when the selection process was announced, it was stated that applicants would need to have been in post as a detective inspector for at least a year. I would have had ten months in post by this time; I was therefore barred from applying. I regarded this as unfair. My promotion had been delayed by a year due to the ramifications of the arrests of corrupt detectives at Rigg. Through no fault of my own, I had 'lost' a year in the rank of detective inspector. I appealed in writing against this unfairness and received a phone call from a deputy assistant commissioner. He informed me that I was merely unlucky – as unlucky as someone who had spent time in hospital with a broken leg and therefore missed out on the promotion process.

At this point, I became angry. The delay had

been caused by me being brave enough to confront police corruption. Also, during my time with the Anti-Terrorist Branch, I had been an acting detective inspector for over a year and had also been involved in police activities far beyond my rank. I suggested that this should contribute towards my time as a detective inspector. This deputy assistant commissioner refused to listen to me. My actions as a whistle-blower received no recognition from the Met. I did not expect any recognition, but then again, perhaps some slight allowance of maybe two months could have been made for me? Could there have not been recognition of the science degree that I had just recently achieved? There was, after all, a provision in the appeal system for candidates with exceptional circumstances. Obviously, I was not exceptional enough!

When I did achieve the requisite year in post to apply for promotion, the goalposts were now moved upwards to two years in post as a detective inspector. I now had to wait two years before applying. I fell slightly short of the two-year requirement and had to wait almost another year until the new promotion process began again. By now, I had almost three years in post.

My written application to the senior management at Haringey was successful. I attended the selection centre at Beak Street in

Central London. For this interview, I would be anonymous, and the selection panel would have no idea about my past. I was just a number and not a name.

All promotion candidates were officially made aware that the first question from the interview panel would be to describe an example of 'decision-making'. As I was seated in the interview room, I vaguely recognised one of the two on the selection panel as a senior detective from East London. I became slightly uneasy. When asked, I described to the panel my example of decision-making. My supervisors had approved my example during my written application, stating it was a valid example of decision-making. The response from the senior detective on the panel was that I had not given a valid example of decision-making. I pointed out that it met the necessary criteria. He shook his head and asked for another example. I had a second example to hand. My supervisors had also approved this example during the written application as being valid. Again, he said that I had not given a valid example of decision-making. I was asked further questions but met with hostility. Unsurprisingly, I failed this interview.

I then commenced an appeal against the unfairness of this promotion interview. I was met with official resistance all along the way. Eventually, under close supervision, I was permitted to view the interview notes made by both members of the panel during my interview. The panel had accurately noted my examples, but against both examples of decision-making, they had noted that they were not valid. I could not understand how they had reached this decision. No explanation was given to me during my appeal explaining the panel's perverse decision. The names of the two members of the interview panel were refused to me when I asked for them.

The following year, I again attended the selection centre for promotion to chief inspector. This time, I spoke very slowly so that the panel would fully note my example of decision-making. However, I spoke so slowly that I ran out of time for the panel to ask questions. This counted against me for marks. I failed the assessment by only 2%.

I decided to no longer bother with promotion, although I had been an acting detective chief inspector for two years at Tottenham in Haringey. This was possibly the most demanding position in the country for a DCI, and I was successful in this role. As I had an 'acting' role, I did not receive any extra pay.

The Borough of Haringey was geographically

split regarding crime. To the west, the population was mainly wealthy, and crime was low. Celebrities such as Sting had a residence here. To the east, crime was high. The dividing line was Green Lanes, which ran from the North Circular Road and into central London. Politically, voters to the west were Liberal Democrats, whereas those to the east were staunch Labour voters.

The population of Haringey Borough was about 250,000, and there were over one hundred and sixty different languages spoken. It was probably the most diverse borough in London. (There are thirty-two London boroughs). The police borough of Haringey had about six hundred and fifty police officers. Of course, not all of these officers are on duty every day. On a good day, there would be about twenty-five uniform officers available at any one time to deal with emergency calls, plus a multitude of other commitments. That is equivalent to one uniform officer per ten thousand of the Haringey population. Those twenty-five available officers could be halved in numbers within a few hours due to the arrests that they had made. Even the simplest of arrests can take six hours to deal with.

The politicians would say that the ratio is better than that; it is not. Many of the Met's

32,000 officers are assigned to specialist units such as the CID, riot control, public demonstrations, diplomatic protection units, and firearm units. Plus, more than a third will be off duty or at court at any one time. Further losses are to training courses and sickness.

A further loss to police numbers is never mentioned: computers have dragged police officers from the streets to sit in front of a screen for hours. For instance, reporting a burglary used to involve filling in an A5-sized sheet of paper. This would then be attached to a ring-binder for a CID officer to investigate. Filling in the blanks would take about ten minutes. Now, the officer is required to spend thirty minutes or more at a computer screen filling in the many fields. I would say that there has been a 25% reduction in police numbers due to the 'advances' of information technology. Certain offences such as muggings created an army of pen-pushers analysing the data, hoping to produce what was expected to be a 'nugget' of intelligence that would crack open unsolvable cases. These 'nuggets' were never found. Senior officers of high rank continued to be taken in by this crazy philosophy for over twenty years. It was decided that almost 5% of borough police officers had to be employed in the role of analysing all the crimes to produce these 'nuggets'. It was all due to information technology – the false prophet of hope.

The only 'nuggets' produced after days of digital number-crunching were descriptions matching exactly that as provided by the victims in the first place. Very, very occasionally, a name would be suggested. This name would always be a known criminal but with nothing evidential to justify arresting them. How on Earth were the police going to get anywhere with just a name? The suggestion was that the criminal would be arrested, and the evidence somehow found. Perhaps there would be a confession? How likely is that with the solicitor sitting next to them, advising them to provide 'no comment' answers? So, with the excessive demands of computers and 5% of officers posted 9 to 5 analysing crime information, how was the public being best served?

Supposedly, the answer to this dilemma was to employ covert surveillance. The theory was that if the intelligence unit had named a possible burglar, a surveillance team would follow them for twenty-four hours a day for a week and hopefully catch them in the act. However, surveillance teams were almost impossible to acquire. These teams had other priorities, such as terrorism, murder, and rape to deal with. A Haringey burglar was therefore not a priority. Very occasionally, a surveillance team could become available but only for a day or two at best. Often, they would be diverted away from Haringey at the last moment. So, we had so many at their desks chasing an occasional nugget of intelligence but no resources to improve upon it. Due to health and safety requirements, Haringey police officers were not permitted to form a surveillance team of their own. Extensive training was a requirement of health and safety legislation to become a surveillance officer, but this training was not available for borough officers.

As an aside, the head of Haringey Council is not only paid far more than the head of Haringey police but also paid far more than the prime minister. This applies to the heads of all thirty-two London boroughs. Also, the head of Haringey Council can veto the selection of a particular chief superintendent to head up the borough. Shortly after I retired, I had a meeting with the then-chief superintendent of Haringey borough. He was the police commander. I wanted to discuss the role of Haringey Council CCTV and its total lack of success in fighting crime. He vehemently disagreed with me, stating that the Council system was wonderful and the police had a marvellous working relationship with them. Of course, he had to say that the head of Haringey Council out-ranked him and could adversely influence his career if he said otherwise. I reminded him that, in the seven years before I retired, Haringey Council CCTV had only once been useful in providing evidence against a criminal. My comment to him fell upon deaf ears.

I lived in Surrey for two years after I retired. I spoke with the head of the CCTV Council system that related to the town of Walton-on-Thames. I asked him for examples of when the cameras had resulted in the arrest of an offender. He said that this was not the role of CCTV. He went on to tell me that their CCTV was there to provide public reassurance. Obviously, this was 'management speak' to say that there had been no arrests.

I mentioned earlier that I took the lead nationally with video evidence. I was a member of two senior officer national police groups, even though I was only a detective sergeant at that time. I also devised and adapted London CCTV systems to help defeat any terrorist threat. One such system was instrumental in solving a murder in its first few weeks. I now decided that it would be best to put my experience to good use in Haringey. My target would be street crime (mugging). This was an offence common to the east of Haringey. It was not unusual to record more than ten muggings in a day.

What exactly is a 'mugging'? In legal terms, it

is a robbery and offence under the 1968 Theft Act. In essence, a robbery is theft, where at the time of the 'mugging', force or the threat of force is used against a person to steal.

The usual method for street robberies (muggings) to be committed is when someone is walking alone in the street and is approached by one or more males who stop their victim and threaten them with a knife or knives. They then demand that the wallet/purse/bag and phone be handed over. I have seen robberies take place on a video recording, and they are hardly noticeable to the casual observer: no overt threats can be seen, and passers-by fail to notice the event. The mugging can be over in a few seconds.

The victim then looks around for help. They now have no phone and head home to contact the police. What can the police do? The muggers have long since gone from the crime scene. The description of the muggers gives skin colour and clothing. Police officers in the area (if there are any available) will be given these details, but among a thousand or more people out on the street, what are the chances of them being arrested? No chance at all is the answer.

One police tactic was to arrange for the victim of the robbery to be driven around in a police car with the hope of spotting the muggers. Very rarely was this successful. Assuming the victim spotted a gang that they genuinely believed had mugged them, police units would have to be found to assist in the arrests. The CPS would probably cast doubt upon the accuracy of the identification. The cost of diverting police officers with little chance of success for this tactic was questionable. To further complicate matters, many muggings never happened and were simply insurance frauds. I suspect that about 10% to 15% of muggings were made up to claim insurance for a lost phone. About another 10% involved gangs, where one gang member mugged another to recover what was probably a drug debt. The victim would then refuse to help the CID. The truth was very elusive at times. If a mugger was arrested, the victim would often decide not to help the police any further as they feared retribution.

So, what about Haringey Council CCTV? Could this help? Haringey Council had a manned CCTV system, which cost over a hundred thousand pounds to run every year. Their camera operators stared at about twenty screens at a time but never spotted a mugging or any other crime. Out of interest, I tried being a CCTV operator in the Council CCTV control room. Within ten minutes, I had lost all concentration trying to follow all the screens at once. It was exhausting. In my seven years as a detective inspector at Haringey, the Council

CCTV system did not spot a single mugging or assault. It spotted only a single crime in seven years. But they certainly persecuted motorists for minor infringements, earning the Council many thousands every year in fines. About ten operators were employed looking for traffic offences, and only two were employed to look for crime. The council managers stated that if an operator saw a crime about to happen, the ten operators looking for traffic offences would divert their attention to look for the criminals. The flaw in this statement was that the crime operators never spotted any crimes occurring in the first place.

I therefore decided that the only effective way to deal with muggers was to create my own police CCTV system. Why? As I mentioned earlier when discussing my Anti-Terrorist Branch years, video evidence can be better than DNA and fingerprints. The video evidence must be of high quality to achieve this. It must also be of sufficient quality to convince a jury that the man in the dock is the same as the man in the video. The jury must be convinced beyond all reasonable doubt. That is the law. The Met police, of course, did not have the finances to build a CCTV control room to match that of Haringey Council or anything like it. My plan was to build a CCTV system that was cheap but effective. I had an idea.

To identify a mugger, I needed a close-up video shot. Haringey Council videos were very wide-angled, and everyone in view was the size of a small ant at best. Yes, the Council camera operators could zoom in, but they never did. Why? Because there was nothing to attract their attention. As I pointed out, muggers do not want to attract attention.

Here is an interesting point: a victim of a mugging can always be exact as to where they were mugged. They can also give the time and how many mugged them. They can give a description of their clothes, skin colour, and in which direction they made off. Most muggings took place in a main street, such as Tottenham High Road. So, there is no need to record the mugging in useless wide-angle: just place a few cameras at one-hundred-yard intervals, focused on a small section of the pavement. The cameras would record 24/7 and not need a human presence. The cameras could also be sited above ground in shop storerooms and focused on the pavement across the street. Muggers would have to pass through the narrow and concentrated beams of these cameras at some point on the way to a mugging and on the way back. After a mugging, all that was needed was for police officers to check the recordings of cameras nearest to the muggings against the description of the muggers. Lo and behold, the muggers would be seen walking through the camera beam just before and just after the mugging. The cameras were 'video-turnstiles' through which all pedestrians had to pass.

I first tested this with just one camera located in Bruce Grove on Tottenham High Road. Within a couple of days, a mugging took place about twenty-five yards away from the narrow focus of the camera. The mugger walked through the narrow beam and was recorded in full detail from head to toe. His body almost filled the screen. He was identified straight away as a known criminal. The next job was to find him. But before we could, he was killed in a road accident.

I realised that the system had potential. Shortly afterwards, I attended a meeting at New Scotland Yard to discuss 'muggings' and tactics available to the police. The meeting was attended by detectives drawn from across the Met and chaired by Deputy Assistant Commissioner Bill Griffiths – he had been my DCI when I was a detective constable at West Ham. In the lunch break, I approached him with my new idea for a video system. In the presence of several colleagues who I had known for years, I told him that I had a new idea that would result in the arrest of many muggers. Those gathered with me were amazed at my daring. They took one step back to await a response from Bill Griffiths. They had no idea about what I was to say. Bill looked slightly taken aback, and I could see that he was wondering if I was being serious or not. I outlined my concept for a video system, and he was very interested. He saw the potential of it and gave me his support. This support gave me credibility in funding the system, which would not be cheap. Bill Griffiths was a natural leader and a cut far above almost all his colleagues in the senior ranks.

Haringey police only had two video cameras and recorders suitable for this role. I had to find many more to make the system work across the borough. Where could I find the money to buy them? I raided every budget that I could find in the Met to purchase cameras and recorders. Ironically, Haringey Council also provided money to buy cameras and equipment.

I named the system the Video Sentry Unit (VSU). I was fortunate to have two uniform officers working in plain clothes to assist me. One had been a member of the Parachute Regiment and served in the Falklands War at Goose Green and other engagements. He was a very steady character, totally reliable, and an inspiration to others. The other was a university graduate with scientific qualifications. He had been accepted as an army officer after university but decided to opt for a career in the police. He was inventive regarding supporting the system and was also a great asset. These officers were not interested in promotion, and both have now retired as police constables. Most police officers are not interested in promotion and see higher ranks as having escaped the front line due to their incompetence. The resentment towards senior officers is quite profound. Even today, the police nationally need to abandon quotas and seek out the best. The police need leaders, not managers.

Within a year, I had about sixty cameras operating across Haringey borough. Within two years, there were one hundred and twenty cameras. The VSU had its own dedicated office for viewing and storing recordings; each recording was kept for a month. The cameras were deployed in crime 'hot-spots'. In other words, I put them where muggings and other serious crimes happened. Dozens of muggers were now being arrested and convicted at court. I saw this system as being useful nationally in the fight against crime. It sounds odd now, but I was the first in the Met to use digital technology. I had been advised that digital technology was open to abuse and could be discredited by the courts. However, the industry was using digital technology, and courts accepted it. I decided to use digital technology, and the Met followed my example. The VSU system did not require the legal restrictions imposed on a conventional police surveillance camera because the cameras were not targeting a specific individual, nor were they specifically focused on a private address. The system was, in effect, a CCTV system with static cameras and without expensive and inefficient operators.

As an experiment, the VSU camera hard drives covering Wood Green High Road were removed and a twenty-four-hour segment was viewed. This was done just to see if any other criminal incidents were occurring that had not been reported to the police. The results were shocking. Gang fights were found to have occurred on High Road, where baseball bats and metal bars were used. Members of the public could be seen scattering in all directions. Nothing regarding this was reported to the police. Other assaults appeared to have happened between young adult males.

In 2001, I was selected for secondment to the government (Home Office) to assist in creating national police technology projects. The Home Office organisation I was seconded to was the Police Information Technology Organisation (PITO). My role was to be an information technology consultant. My police experience was of value in that I could advise whether a particular technological project was likely to be of practical value to the police. I expected that the Home Office would support my Video Sentry Unit innovation nationally. I was wrong. Despite being considered by their highest authority, it was not supported, and no valid reason was provided to me. Perhaps the government preferred their own home-grown projects to mine?

PITO no longer exists and has been replaced by a similar Home Office organisation. The concept of this organisation was valid: there were forty-three police forces in England and Wales, and each was independent as far as the purchase of information technology was concerned. As a result, there was no national coordination regarding the purchase of information technology. Each force purchased software that could not often 'talk' to the software of adjoining forces. Forces were also often sold systems that, on the surface, appeared to be competitively priced but ended up being locked into highly expensive maintenance contracts for years.

My office was in a building close to Blackfriars Bridge and on the south bank of the River Thames. Although I only lived ten miles away at that time, it took ninety minutes to get there via car, the underground, and walking.

Much of my week was spent on the road visiting police scientific staff at police force HQs around the country and attending meetings.

Most of my colleagues were civilians who were specialists in their chosen areas of expertise. All had scientific qualifications, and a number were also there as consultants. I found them to be friendly, approachable, and hard-working. However, the decision-making process was slow when compared to my policing experience. Their world revolved around meetings, committees, and yet more meetings. I had devised and instigated the Video Sentry Unit on my own with the help of only two police officers. I scavenged funding wherever I could. Unlike the Home Office, I did not have the luxury of a project leader, project manager, or assistant project manager, plus a dozen members of the project team.

My frustrations at the slow pace of progress boiled over one afternoon. For the previous three Friday afternoons, I and my colleagues were required to attend presentations trying to motivate us in the workplace. The presentations were provided by a team of consultants from an external agency at some cost. At the start of the presentation, we all had to clap ourselves for having worked so hard during the week. Really? Next, the speaker would ask if we had any good news to share with everyone. Someone put his hand up and explained that his young daughter had come home after school with an Easter egg engraved with his name on it. This made him happy. The speaker then asked us all to clap for this good news before asking if anyone else had any good news that could be shared. I put my hand up. "Yes, Bob, what's your good news that you can share with us?" I put on my serious voice and said, "My wife died on Tuesday evening without any warning. It was completely unexpected". You could hear a pin drop. I then paused before putting my happy face on. "But the good news is that I get her full life insurance pay-out on Saturday!" The shocked expression on the speaker's face was well worth the effort. My police line manager took me to one side after this session and expressed his concern about my 'inappropriate' humour. More fool him, I thought to myself. Everyone else found it to be amusing.

Most police officers seconded to PITO were from outside the Met. They were able to claim all the London police allowances and had a chance to retire on a Met pension. Most were compliant and knew their place. Why would they want to rock the boat and lose all those allowances and an enhanced pension? I was not compliant.

One of the best PITO projects was a national automated fingerprint system supplied to each police force. This system took an electronic image of an arrested person's fingerprints and immediately compared them with fingerprint records held at New Scotland Yard. It was therefore easy to immediately identify if the arrested person had a criminal history and if they were wanted for questioning about an offence or had absconded from prison. In the past, fingerprints were taken with a manual roller and ink; no immediate comparison with records held at New Scotland Yard was possible until the forms arrived in the internal mail a few days later. Within those few days, the arrested person would probably have been released if a false name had been given.

A frustrating part of fingerprint evidence was that the UK required high-quality fingerprint evidence before it could be used in court. Europe and the USA, for instance, did not require such high quality of evidence. This quality was based upon the number of tiny ridges that can be seen on each fingerprint. In the UK, it could be possible to match a fingerprint found at the scene of a burglary with a criminal's fingerprint, but it may not have been of sufficient quality to use it as evidence. However, the same fingerprint would have been sufficient to use in European and USA courts.

I discovered that one Home Office project had a serious flaw; the flaw was not seen as a problem by the Home Office. They were wrong. This flaw severely limited the scope for the investigation of serious crime. I took this matter very seriously and, without authority from the Home Office, presented my concerns at New Scotland Yard to over two hundred high-ranking Met detectives. This did not go down well with the Home Office. The following Monday, I was sent back to Haringey police for 'administrative reasons' after less than two years into my secondment. I was not surprised, and it was a relief to return to the real world of frontline policing.

At this time, there was a senior police officer at management board level who was interested in employing the Video Sentry Unit Met-wide. However, he told me there was no police funding available to do this. Undeterred, I therefore sought funding elsewhere. I was advised by a commander at New Scotland Yard to approach Ellie Roy, head of the Government Office for London for funding. This organisation was extremely influential. It represented central government across London and the southeast of England. They worked towards making London a better place. She invited me to provide a presentation on the VSU to her team. My presentation was warmly received, and she granted funding for the Video Sentry Unit to be replicated on each of the thirty-two boroughs throughout the Met.

My joy was short-lived; things then started to go wrong for me. The senior police officer at management board level I mentioned now became very annoyed with me. He decided to turn down the funding for the Video Sentry system offered by Ellie Roy. One early morning before I had left home, he phoned me and angrily told me that I had been "rowing my own boat" without his permission. Before I could respond, he terminated the call. In other words, I had damaged his ego by speaking with Ellie Roy without his authority. I repeatedly tried to ring him back, but his secretary blocked my calls. He then commenced 'discipline proceedings' against me. This could have resulted in the loss of my job, demotion, or a heavy fine. Interestingly, no police officer in his chain of command would act against me. It was eventually devolved to a uniform officer of one rank above me who courageously ended the process by writing that I had done nothing wrong and was simply seeking extra funding.

Meanwhile, the Video Sentry Unit went from strength to strength in its success against not just muggers but also other criminals. One example was a man from Wood Green who heard voices in his head, telling him to attack Christians. He was a Turkish Muslim. This was at Christmas, and he stabbed three innocent people. The second victim was a woman on a bicycle. He stabbed her in the body with a long knife as she cycled past him on the A10 dual carriageway. She survived. This was not recorded on my cameras. He also stabbed to death an elderly man in Enfield. Later, just off Wood Green High Road, he stabbed a passer-by numerous times. This was recorded in horrific detail on one of my cameras. The CPS intended to charge the attacker with GBH regarding the cyclist and this man, but having seen my video, they charged him with attempted murder for both. Attempted Murder charges are rare as a substantial amount of evidence is needed to provide intent to murder. My video provided evidence of this intent.

Another example was a murder with a gun by a gang. A gang was recorded in detail on one of my cameras. They approached the victim while he sat in his car and shot him dead. The video evidence convicted them all at the Old Bailey. There was no lengthy trial lasting weeks and costing many thousands of pounds. The savings to the taxpayer were proving to be enormous. Crimes were being solved very cheaply, and all the criminals were accepting their guilt at court as the video evidence was perfect. The cost of a

Crown Court is over £5,000 daily. These crimes were dealt with in one day instead of the usual three weeks. Also, the crimes would not have been solved without my video evidence.

Over the years, more than a hundred muggers were arrested and convicted due to my Video Sentry camera evidence. My team would view the recordings of nearby cameras to where the mugging took place and spot the muggers walking through the narrow beam of one or more cameras. The images were so clear that they could be identified and arrested.

Eventually, I had over one hundred and twenty cameras viewing Haringey crime hotspots. These crime hotspots were at Seven Sisters, Tottenham High Road, Bruce Grove, Wood Green High Road, and Muswell Hill High Road. These hotspot areas comprised shops, pubs, and clubs; muggers were always attracted to where the public gathered. Over a five-year period, muggings in Wood Green High Road reduced by 50%. Over nine hundred serious crimes were solved by my CCTV system in ten years. Haringey Council CCTV solved nothing during this period. Additionally, the Video Sentry Unit solved about a hundred times more crimes than the heavily staffed intelligence unit. This was no fault of the police officers and support staff in the unit: they were not supported by a trained surveillance team to develop their findings. The lack of surveillance teams was a Met-wide problem. This was the fault of senior officers who failed to appreciate this serious deficiency. I would raise this subject at meetings, but I would be told by police superintendents that I had a 'glass half-empty' attitude and should be more 'positive'.

On one occasion, I and one of the VSU team took a walk along Wood Green High Road looking for a group of muggers who had clearly been recorded on the VSU cameras. We were not in uniform. We each had a still from one of the recordings to help us spot them. After about twenty minutes of walking back and forth along the High Road, we found them. My colleague had a police radio, and we called for some help. When it arrived, we arrested them all. They were charged with robbery (mugging) and appeared in court. Unfortunately, the person who had been mugged did not turn up at court and could not be found. The case was therefore dropped. He later told us that he was too scared to give evidence as he lived in the locality. This was not an unusual event, but it was very frustrating for the police.

A substantial number of offenders recorded by Video Sentry cameras could not be identified; they were not known to Haringey police officers and had probably travelled from other parts of London or from outside London. So, we would have captured on camera clear facial images of the offenders but could not identify them by name. I approached our media press officer in person and asked if these images could receive media coverage with an appeal for information from the public. The response was that it was only another mugging and not of great public interest. This was extremely frustrating, but there was no way around it. I did arrange for the images to be circulated to other police stations, but we only had some success with this method. It was odd that we had an intelligence unit struggling to find evidence against criminals, yet the Video Sentry Unit was finding substantial evidence daily.

I came to realise that most senior police officers could not grasp how the Video Sentry Unit was so successful. I gave a lecture at New Scotland Yard to all senior officers about how the VSU worked. At the end of my lecture, I detected a lot of blank faces in the audience. I took a deep breath and repeated myself in full.

I did find that I fell between two stools with my Video Sentry Unit. The civilian technical units based at New Scotland Yard viewed me with suspicion verging on hostility. Who was I, they thought, to take on this technical role? The same view was held by many in police senior management. Their view was that I was a detective, not a technician, and I should know my place. My role as the Video Sentry Unit supervisor was an extra responsibility that I had created, and yet I still had to supervise robbery and burglary investigations along with forensic investigations.

This brings me onto the subject of police crime targets as specified by the Home Office with government approval. For instance, the Home Office set a target for the Met of reducing 'muggings' by 5% for the year. Failure to meet this target can result in the loss of bonus pay to senior ranking officers. I was the supervisor for street robbery (muggings) investigations at Haringey. I also was the supervisor for burglary and forensic investigations. With the use of my Video Sentry system to make arrests, street robberies fell by 40%. This made us the best in the Met. However, I was criticised by senior officers for doing this as it would make achieving another 5% reduction the following year almost impossible. Their view was that I should only have reduced muggings by 5% and stopped any further arrests once that had been achieved. By this logic, more members of the public would have been mugged and injured. This was all for the sake of statistics.

These cameras were also able to establish that a huge number of muggings were false reports. If someone lost their phone, they would often report it as a mugging to claim insurance. Examination of adjacent cameras would prove that the victim was not there at the time and that no mugging had taken place. The 'victim' would often then become hard to find. Telling lies to the police was never prosecuted as the fear was that it would discourage the public from contacting the police. The report would still be recorded as a crime, even if the victim could not be traced or refused to cooperate with the police investigation. Some of those who reported being mugged said that the muggers returned their sim card when asked. As if they would!

In May 2012, the street artist 'Banksy' was recorded on a Video Sentry Unit camera creating one of his famous secretive murals. His mural was on the wall of a Poundland store in Whymark Road, Wood Green, and was entitled 'Slave Labour'. It was created shortly before the celebrations to mark the queen's Diamond Jubilee. His secret method was clear to see on the video, and so was his face. Senior police officers advised the Video Sentry team not to publicise this finding and keep it secret. I am now the first to mention this publicly. In my view, 'Banksy' had committed a criminal offence by painting on the walls of the council and private property.

This is normally known as graffiti and costs local authorities many thousands of pounds every month to clean up. Anyone else seen doing this would be arrested. Why did senior police officers provide him with exemption to the law? Upon whose authority were they acting? Is this corruption?

I created the Video Sentry Unit with the primary aim of reducing muggings. Although successful in this aim, other unexpected offences were solved. One such was a report of male rape. This male reported to his boyfriend that he was late home because he had been raped. According to his written statement to the investigating detective, two men had coerced him to walk with them from Seven Sisters tube station along High Road. They had then allegedly forced him behind a builder's skip in a car park where the alleged offence had taken place. Male rape is as serious as female rape but not as common. The higher command at New Scotland Yard had taken an interest in the investigation, and there was political pressure to bring the perpetrators to justice.

The VSU studied their recordings from the vicinity of the Seven Sisters tube station and along Tottenham High Road. They saw the victim walking with two men on numerous cameras. However, he was following behind the two men and talking to them as they walked. There were no signs of a struggle. The men then paused together, and all three walked behind a builder's skip and out of sight. Shortly afterwards, all three men emerged into view. They stood chatting to each other for a minute or so before splitting up. When confronted with the recordings, the victim changed his story and admitted that no rape had taken place. He made his false account as an excuse to his boyfriend for being late. This discovery saved the police thousands of pounds in wasted hours looking for two non-existent rapists. It would also have been necessary to warn tube travellers that two rapists were prowling the trains looking for victims. This would have caused unnecessary distress to travellers.

Forensic evidence is vital. In my opinion, forensic scene examiners and scientists are the new detectives. A good example of this was the investigation of the alleged rape of a fifteen-year-old girl in Haringey. She had been missing from home for a week, and when she returned home, she told her parents that she had been raped. She also provided the name of the teenage rapist to the police in her written statement. The teenage rapist was a known criminal with criminal convictions. He was arrested and admitted having sex with the girl but with her consent. He said that no rape occurred. The investigation then became rather complicated. Swabs were taken from the girl and submitted for forensic analysis. The result from the analysis of the swabs showed that she'd had sex with numerous men over a period of a few days. This result contradicted her written account. In fact, she had attended numerous parties during the time she was away from home, and sexual intercourse with her consent had taken place with many men. Obviously, there was insufficient evidence for a rape prosecution.

The Video Sentry Unit was unintentionally disbanded by the then-Met commissioner in 2013 and after I had retired from the Met. He decided that all video cameras should be stored at New Scotland Yard in case of a terrorist attack. The cameras were removed from their positions in Haringey crime hot spots and taken to New Scotland Yard for storage. This commissioner was known not to tolerate dissent, and no senior officer from Haringey would dare challenge his decision. The logic of his thinking escapes me, even to this day. Was he pointlessly intending to surround a bomb crater with cameras after a terrorist explosion? As far as I am aware, the cameras are still stored somewhere in New Scotland Yard and were never used.

My Video Sentry CCTV system was not the only responsibility I had. I was on call for one week in six. The week I was on call as the duty detective inspector was for 24/7 during the week. I had to respond to serious incidents during the night as well as during the day. Quite often, I had to work during the night and continue the next day. There was no overtime for me. Inspectors and above were not granted overtime payments.

One afternoon at about 4 pm, I was called to the recreation ground next to the Broadwater Farm in Tottenham. The recreation ground is a large, public open space, like a municipal park. A man in his twenties had been found dead near some bushes. By the initial assessment by the uniform inspector and forensic examiner, it was believed that death had been caused by a drug overdose. When I inspected the scene, I decided that this was a probable murder and for the following reasons: the young man had no shoes, and in my opinion, had fled from the Broadwater Farm, which was about two hundred yards away, possibly to escape a violent assault. He was not wearing an outer jacket despite it being a very cold day. There were no discarded shoes nearby; he was smartly dressed and certainly not a vagrant. I did not approach the body as it is always best to forensically preserve the crime scene as much as possible. Having declared the incident to be a probable murder, I arranged for the scene to be cordoned off and deployed officers to search for witnesses and make a note of all cars and CCTV in the vicinity. Homicide detectives from New Scotland Yard attended shortly after, and I briefed them as to my conclusions. Some of them were concerned about the nearby presence of the Broadwater Farm and its history. To me, the Broadwater Farm was no more dangerous than many other areas of London. The homicide team doctor examined the body and found stab wounds to his back. These had resulted in small puncture wounds to the chest. These small puncture wounds had, previously to my arrival, been wrongly assessed as being from a hypodermic needle used in drug abuse. My murder assessment had been correct.

Had I agreed with the initial crime scene assessment that it was simply a drug overdose, the body would have been taken away to a morgue pending a routine post-mortem several days later. Only then would the pathologist have discovered that it was a murder. The loss of more than 24 hours of investigation time would have been evidentially catastrophic, and the chances of a successful murder investigation would have been hugely diminished. Not only would the murderers have remained free to kill again, but closure would not have been brought to the victim's family. It was established that the victim had answered the door of his flat on the

Broadwater Farm, where his killers attacked him with knives. He managed to run away for a short distance across the park before he succumbed to his wounds. The killers were arrested and convicted of murder at the Old Bailey.

At about this time, I was given a slightly odd and risky assignment by the chief superintendent of Haringey police. There was a rock concert at Finsbury Park, which was attended by thousands of people. I was wearing a suit and tie; the chief superintendent was in full uniform. I was driving him around the area of the concert when we passed a pub close to the venue and busy with drinkers overflowing onto the pavement. He asked me to stop our car. We both stepped out, and he suggested we walk up to the pub. We were in plain view to all the drinkers outside as we approached. When we were about ten yards away, he stopped and told me to go into the pub and keep my ears open for any loose talk. So, he was expecting me to blend into the background and eavesdrop on the surrounding conversations? Unsurprisingly, space appeared for me at the bar. I decided that my best option was to order a pint of Guinness, followed by another. I left in a happier state of mind but gathered no information.

A senior officer at Haringey police decided that a good way to increase arrests and convictions for drug possession would be to have a drug detector dog at Seven Sisters tube station. The dog would sniff passengers as they entered and left the underground booking hall. The police officers with the dog would then process those detained. It was a good idea, but it was doomed to failure. When the statistics appeared on the computer screens at Scotland Yard, there was uproar. Why had Haringey now become a hotbed of drug misuse overnight? asked the very senior officers. The spike in the statistics was viewed as a failure of command. To make matters worse, the credit for all the arrests was passed over to British Transport Police (BTP). The booking hall was BTP territory and not part of the Met.

Quite often, an investigation could slip out of control and become, without justification, a major enquiry, which drained police resources. An example of this was a report concerning a nine-year-old girl on her way to school in Haringey. She had been seen by a member of the public to be fighting off a man about fifty yards from her school gates. This was treated as a possible attempted abduction with the potential of serious consequences to the girl. I went to the alleged crime scene. The supposed abduction would have been in view of dozens of school children and their parents. The Haringey senior officers decided that this should be investigated by Haringey police. I objected to this; although there were indications that the witness could have been mistaken, it was wrong in my view to use the limited resources of Haringey police when we could call upon specialist teams to help. My view was accepted, and New Scotland Yard was contacted.

It transpired that the girl's father had been having a friendly tussle with his daughter at the exact point where the witness had seen them. Furthermore, his description and that of the girl matched the details the witness provided. Both were described by the witness as being of East Asian appearance. Additionally, no girls were missing from the school. This would now have been the time to close the investigation. However, it was decided by more senior officers that the investigation would continue, just in case there was an actual abduction of another girl at the same spot and time and with the same description. There was a severe lack of decision-making skills exhibited by senior officers. I did not make myself popular by pointing out how ridiculous it was to continue with this charade. When the investigation eventually ended and there was certainly no abduction in the first place, we were told that the police response had been a huge success and of reassurance to the public. However, the media had been informed and broadcasted the initial mistaken report as factual. Parents were now terrified for their children and certainly not reassured.

It was always a disappointment to me how members of the public would ignore crime rather than do anything to stop it. If the public acted when even a minor crime was taking place, the country would be much safer. Ironically, I think that the public fear they would be in trouble with the police if they intervened. This fear is unfounded but genuinely held. As an example, I was waiting for a train. About a dozen male commuters were stood around on the platform. A boy of about fifteen years of age was sitting on one of the benches near the entrance. Suddenly, a gang of four boys about his age appeared and attacked him. I was about thirty yards away and ran towards the attackers past six or seven commuters who just stood there watching. The attackers saw me and ran off. The boy on the bench was bleeding from his nose and had a bruised eye. I asked him why he had been attacked, and he just shrugged; he didn't want any police action and said he would sort it out later. Why hadn't the other men on the platform intervened?

Shootings in Haringey happened quite frequently and were often frustratingly difficult to investigate. Most occurred between rival gang members and often only came to the notice of the police when North Middlesex hospital contacted us to say they had patients in casualty with gunshot wounds. We had a general rule of thumb regarding the survivability of gang members from such wounds: in essence, the more criminal convictions the patient had for crime, the greater his chance of surviving. This seemed to be the rule. So, we now had a gang member in hospital. Our duty was to investigate and prevent a repetition. We'd speak to the gang member, and he would claim to have seen nothing and that he was the subject of a random attack with no description of the assailant. We would seize his clothing for forensic purposes.

The location that he'd give of the shooting would be very vague and impossible to pin down. Obviously, despite the detectives' best efforts, this investigation would go nowhere. Many police hours would be wasted going through the investigative process. Furthermore, our gang member would disappear from his hospital bed before his treatment had ended. He would, of course, survive this reckless action and continue with his criminal activities. It was said that the staff of the North Middlesex hospital were the most experienced in the country at dealing with gunshot and knife wounds.

I had quite a close call with one of these gangland shootings. One Friday afternoon, as I sat in my office preparing to go home, I heard a succession of loud bangs nearby. I had heard gunshots when I was in the military; these were certainly gunshots and not a car backfiring. I picked up my large hard-backed notebook for protection and stepped into the street. I saw clouds of gun smoke in the air drifting towards me. I was the first police officer on scene. The parked cars a few yards away had smashed windows from bullets, and the adjacent car showroom's glass frontage had been shattered. Several people were cowering under cars. I was then joined by uniform police officers.

I entered the garage and showroom with armed officers, who quickly arrived on the scene. This was to ensure that the area was safe and to secure evidence. We found an abandoned hold-all bag containing a revolver and a large quantity of ammunition. We were later informed that the shootout was between a Turkish and Jamaican gang over a drug dispute. Later that day, a hospital in South London treated two men. One had severe bruising to his chest, and one had a wound to his ankle. The doctor who treated them had had extensive medical experience in South Africa treating gunshot wounds. In his opinion, the bruises to the chest were caused by the impact of a bullet on body armour. He assessed the foot injury as being from a bullet. These two patients denied having any connection with our Haringey shooting or any shooting at all.

For almost three years during my six year-posting with Haringey police, I was promoted to the rank of acting detective chief inspector. There was no extra pay for this 'acting' role, but with it came the responsibilities. However, I found it to be an easier rank to perform than detective inspector. I found the rank of a detective inspector easier than detective sergeant. I had found the rank of detective sergeant easier than detective constable. The hardest workers in the police are the constables in uniform and the CID. They are continually on the front line and have no idea what dangers they will face when they are next on duty. But, despite this, they are a happy breed and a band of brothers.

I went to a leaving do for a uniform police constable from Tottenham. It was held in a Wetherspoon's pub in Enfield. I was the only police officer there of a rank above PC. By 10 pm, I was confronted by many of the officers pointing their fingers at me and sounding off their dissatisfaction with senior management. I understood their frustrations. If things had gone wrong and there had been a fight, I would have been held to account due to my rank. There was a rule in the Royal Navy for officers when they went ashore and were invited for a drink with the sailors. The advice was to have just one drink and then leave. Perhaps they were right.

There were about six hundred and fifty police officers in Haringey borough. I was outranked by about eight officers, and most were in uniform.

It was demoralising to often deal with officers who had been promoted beyond their experience and ability. One such case was a female uniform inspector who phoned me to seek help. One of the constables she was supervising had attended Wood Green Crown Court and had suffered adverse criticism from the prosecuting barrister at his lack of preparation for the court case. The barrister quite rightly wished to speak with his supervisor and communicate his concerns. However, this inspector was terrified of attending Crown Court: she had never been and felt that I should go instead. I explained to her that all she had to do was meet with the barrister at Court and listen to his concerns. I told her that I was very busy, and she would have to take the responsibility that went with her rank. I then terminated the conversation. She was the same rank as me. Later that day, I received a phone call from my boss requesting that I attend Crown Court in her place. Her boss had complained to the chief superintendent, who took her side. I'm sure that if the uniform inspector had been male, he would have had no such support. Senior police officers were terrified of accusations of sexism and racism. The same probably applies today.

We at Haringey had been short of a detective inspector for some months. The adverse effect was that we had to provide night-duty cover more often. Night-duty was always onerous as it had to be combined with our day-duty tasks and always resulted in a lack of sleep. However, we were informed that an experienced detective inspector from the fraud squad at New Scotland Yard was to join us and make up the numbers. The day arrived when this experienced detective inspector joined us, and I couldn't help but notice that she was six months pregnant and about to go on maternity leave. While she was away, we were not entitled to a replacement, as in theory, the vacancy had been filled. Police officers are entitled to take up to fifteen months of paid maternity leave. This is not a criticism of the woman – she turned out to be very capable and competent – it was the system at fault. No doubt the fraud squad was pleased that she transferred to us as it allowed them to apply for a full-time replacement detective inspector.

Later, we were again short of a detective

inspector on the borough. A detective inspector from Thames Valley police was interested in joining us. He had three years' police service left before he retired. His intention was to join the Met for his last three years and retire on a Met pension. At that time, the Met pension would have been worth several thousand pounds extra per year to him on his Thames Valley pension. He joined us for a day to see how life was for a detective inspector in Haringey. I was nominated to show him around the area and give him an insight as to what would be expected of him. He was noticeably subdued during this drive around. I, of course, included a personal tour of the Broadwater Farm. He left early that day, and we heard nothing more from him.

We later had a detective inspector posted to us from outside the Met. As I mentioned earlier, there was some animosity from members of the police in other forces based upon prejudice and ignorance of the facts. However, this detective inspector didn't carry such baggage and was willing to learn. He found his new role very taxing. He could not sleep at home when on standby for a week's night-duty cover. In fact, he was so restless that he had to sleep in a separate room to his wife. He also committed the cardinal sin of bringing a Tupperware box containing his lunch to work. Met detectives don't do Tupperware.

Additionally, he had a small daily allowance comprising a few coins in a man-purse provided by his wife for tea and coffee. This allowance was insufficient to provide for a round of teas or coffee. Apparently, he said to the other detective inspectors that if he could win my approval, he would know that he had been accepted. Every Monday morning, we detective inspectors and our boss, the detective chief inspector, had a meeting in the senior officer's canteen to discuss the crimes committed during the previous week. This meeting included a briefing from the detective inspector who had been on night-duty for the week. On the Monday morning following his first on-call night duty, our new detective inspector opened a large notebook and began to brief us in detail of every crime that had occurred overnight during that week in Haringey. I intervened very quickly, explaining to him that we only needed to know about murders, rapes, and shootings. He took my point; he'd had a baptism of fire and went on to do well.

All too often and for no specific reason, a Haringey criminal had 'he may have access to a firearm' on his intelligence file. In my view, every criminal in Haringey 'may have access to a firearm'. It certainly didn't mean they had a gun to hand or were willing to use it against police officers. Realistically, knives are as deadly as firearms. But, because a firearm reference had somehow appeared on a criminal's file, it became difficult to arrest him in a pre-planned operation unless a police firearms team was employed to assist. One example typifies the operational dilemmas that this creates. A criminal was wanted by us for muggings, but it was mentioned on his intelligence file that 'he may have access to a firearm'. This meant that we could not arrest him at home without a firearms team being with us.

Firearms teams are extremely professional and based away from Haringey. There is a huge demand on them throughout the Met. The problem was that the firearms teams would only carry out these operations during the early hours, say, 4 am. This would ensure that the suspect was at home in bed and not in a position to resist. The firearms teams did not want a confrontation in the street, as this would put the wider public at risk. The problem for us was that this suspect slept at various addresses during the day and was away at night. So, due to a dubious entry upon his intelligence file, it was not possible to arrest him. I had an idea based on 'practical policing'. There has never been a definition of 'practical policing'. I had a conversation with one of my detective sergeants, who had been on the Flying Squad. (Fortunately, his Flying Squad experience did not relate to

Rigg Approach). He was highly competent, intelligent, and resourceful. He was the man for my 'practical policing'. I told him that we needed a method to overcome the policing logjam created by the suggestion that our suspect had access to a firearm. After a full and frank discussion, I was pleased to note that the following day, our mugger had 'accidentally' collided with the opening door of a CID car as he walked past. No firearm was found on him when he was searched. His home was also searched, but no firearm was found. He was subsequently convicted at court. Had I cut corners? Maybe.

There was a rather bizarre incident involving one of the Video Sentry Unit cameras. Every Monday morning, the Video Sentry team would download the recordings from each of the many cameras on site. When they went to a particular camera and its recorder situated in a storeroom above a shop in Wood Green, they discovered that the camera had been stolen. However, the thieves failed to realise that stealing the camera did not stop the recording. The VSU team replayed the recording, and it showed a man and a woman struggling to remove the camera from its mountings. The images were not clear, but the recorder gave an exact time of the theft, and the images gave a basic but not identifiable description of the thieves. Now, the surrounding

VSU cameras came to our aid. Given the time and basic description of the thieves, the other cameras recorded the thieves carrying the camera away. The thieves were identified and known to us, and they were arrested and convicted at court. The camera was found in a skip and returned to its watchful location.

The London riots of 2011 were widespread and caused much damage and disruption. The epicentre was Tottenham. A criminal named Mark Duggan, who was under surveillance and armed with a gun, had been shot dead by police officers in Ferry Lane. The subsequent independent enquiry found the police officers' actions to be justified. However, in the interests of so-called 'justice', many hundreds of rioters looted and pillaged their way across London. Wood Green High Road and 'Shopping City' in Haringey became a target of the rioters. However, my Video Sentry cameras recorded throughout the looting and provided clear images of the rioters' faces and criminal actions. More than a hundred rioters were arrested over the following year. The investigators were provided with over six hundred hours of footage from the cameras. Without these cameras, there would have been no evidence to justify convictions in court. No other part of London or the UK has or ever had such an effective CCTV system. Had this system been present in all

London boroughs in 2011, there could possibly have been several thousand convictions for rioting. This would probably have ensured no more riots would ever take place in the capital. It was unfortunate that the member of the management board I referred to earlier had denied London the crime fighting asset of a video sentry system in each borough.

There was an interesting investigation involving the Video Sentry Unit concerning Millwall football supporters. Tottenham was due to play Millwall one Saturday afternoon. At about noon, a small group of Millwall supporters attacked The Cockerel pub on Tottenham High Road. This pub was almost opposite Tottenham football ground and seen as being aligned with Tottenham supporters. The timing of the attack was intentional. No police officers would have been deployed until later for a 3 pm kick-off. The attack continued for several minutes. The pub was closed, but extensive damage was caused to the exterior and windows. Nearby road-work rubble was used in the attack. Passers-by were shocked and intimidated. The investigators contacted the Millwall police unit and were able to identify the attackers from the images. Surprisingly perhaps, all the attackers were in their forties and fifties. Most had a history of football-related violence. All appeared at Wood Green Crown Court for trial.

They claimed 'self-defence' as they had felt 'threatened' by the pub!

Here is an example of how far camera technology has progressed in the past twenty years. In 2001, I purchased a particular camera from various funding sources for the Video Sentry Unit. At that time, this camera was revolutionary in that it provided a 20 Mb picture. It used the latest NASA technology and cost thirty-five thousand pounds for one camera. It was positioned on the wall of a bank at a height of twenty feet. Its field of view covered the whole of the plaza at the north end of Wood Green High Road opposite the cinema and shops. It was this camera that solved the murder of a man by a gang with a gun while he was sat in his car. Twenty years later, most mobile phones have a camera that has the capacity to record a 50 Mb picture. This is more than double the capability of the thirty-five thousand pounds camera I bought back in 2001.

As my retirement date approached, I looked forward to it. Although I would only have done twenty-five years' police service rather than thirty, I was ready to leave. I had been granted five years pensionable service from my time with the fire service and the Royal Navy, and this topped up my pensionable service to the required thirty years. The corruption at West

Ham and the subsequent appalling year on the Flying Squad had taken its toll on me. I had also been active on the Anti-Terrorist Branch and fully committed myself to the Video Sentry Unit. There had also been a few murders to solve on the way.

When I came to retire, a new detective inspector was appointed to replace me. He had no CID experience and had decided, as a uniform sergeant, that now would be a good time to become a detective inspector. The CID selection process had gone full circle since I had applied to join the CID. No more was it required that a detective should have experience and ability before progressing through the CID ranks. In fact, delaying my promotion for years to gain CID experience was a waste of time and lost opportunity. Now, any sergeant or inspector could wake up on a Monday morning and decide to be in the CID by the following week. I came to realise that detective inspectors were no longer significant regarding the investigation of serious crime; detective constables performed the real investigation. I often told my detective sergeants that my role was now to sign forms, cull investigations where necessary, and sack dullards. It was the detective sergeants who ran the CID. The shiny and new detective inspector asked me to show him the ropes. I showed him my desk and chair instead. I then left the building forever.

In my first year of retirement, I met with Lynne Featherstone, who was a Member of Parliament for Haringey. I expressed my concerns regarding the performance of the Haringey Council CCTV system. She was supportive. As a result of this meeting, I met with a reporter from the local newspaper, and they produced a front-page covering my concerns. The newspaper requested the Council to produce details of arrests made due to evidence from their CCTV cameras. This request was made under the Freedom of Information Act. The Council refused to provide information as they said the task would have been too time-consuming for them to carry out. This exemption is allowed under the Act. Therefore, no information was forthcoming. In other words, the Council cameras did not assist in any arrests.

I had been divorced four years earlier, and the process had been unpleasant. I was now living in North London. Retirement would give me an opportunity for a fresh start in life. I made that fresh start when I met my future wife, Melanie, in 2010. We now have a son and daughter together. Also living with us is my wife's son from her previous relationship, plus a few cats and dogs.

I have no regrets about joining the Metropolitan Police. It was certainly tough at times but compensated for by working with great colleagues. The consumption of a few barrels of beer along the way did help!

Printed in Great Britain
by Amazon